THE
MIND, BODY, SPIRIT
MISCELLANY

THE
MIND, BODY, SPIRIT
MISCELLANY

*The Ultimate Collection
of Fascinations, Facts, Truths
and Insights*

Jane Alexander

DUNCAN BAIRD PUBLISHERS

LONDON

The Body, Mind, Spirit Miscellany
Jane Alexander

Distributed in the USA and Canada by
Sterling Publishing Co., Inc.
387 Park Avenue South
New York, NY 10016-8810

This edition first published in the UK and USA in 2009 by
Duncan Baird Publishers Ltd
Sixth Floor, Castle House
75–76 Wells Street
London W1T 3QH

Managing Editor: Kirty Topiwala
Editor: Kelly Thompson
Managing Designer: Manisha Patel
Designer: Gail Jones
Commissioned artwork: Colin Elgie and Mark Watkinson

Library of Congress Cataloging-in-Publication Data

Alexander, Jane.
    The body, mind, spirit miscellany : the ultimate collection of fascinations, facts,
truths, and insights / Jane Alexander.
        p. cm.
    ISBN 978-1-84483-837-0
    1. Occultism--Miscellanea. 2. Religions--Miscellanea. I. Title.
    BF1999.A63285 2009
    130--dc22

                                                    2009017592

ISBN: 978-1-84483-837-0
10 9 8 7 6 5 4 3 2 1

Typeset in Garamond
Printed in Finland

For information about custom editions, special sales, premium and corporate
purchases, please contact Sterling Special Sales Department at 800-805-5489 or
specialsales@sterlingpub.com.

Publisher's note: While every care has been taken in compiling the information for
this book, Duncan Baird Publishers, or any other persons who have been involved in
working on this publication, cannot accept responsibility for any errors or omissions,
inadvertent or not, that may be found in the text, nor for any problems, injuries or
damage that may arise as a result of following the advice, exercises, or therapeutic
techniques contained in this book. None of the information or advice is intended as a
substitute for professional medical advice or treatment.

Abbreviations used throughout this book:
CE Common Era (the equivalent of AD)
BCE Before the Common Era (the equivalent of BC)
b. born
d. died

"To the wise, nothing is alien or remote."
ANTISTHENES (c.445BCE–c.365BCE)

"Knowledge is of two kinds. We know a subject ourselves,
or we know where we can find information upon it."
SAMUEL JOHNSON (1709–1784)

"We learn more by looking for the answer to a question
and not finding it than we do from learning the answer itself."
LLOYD ALEXANDER (1924–2007)

A miscellany is a wonderful entity, guaranteed to intrigue and amaze, to amuse and entertain. Who hasn't picked up one intending to read just one entry, only to emerge an hour or so later having been lured into the wonderful world of unusual and unexpected facts? When I was approached to write this book, my first reaction was one of surprise that there wasn't already a miscellany of Mind, Body, Spirit topics. After all, who isn't interested in the net of faith that encircles our world? Who isn't captivated by the curious realm of myth and magic? Who wouldn't like to know how to use natural and unusual remedies to cure everyday complaints? The field is vast – the study not just of life but of the afterlife, too – and in its enormity it can appear daunting for the novice seeker. A miscellany, however, allows you to browse, in a blissfully random way, dipping and delving into a patchwork of enlightening lists, explanations, clarifications, summaries and curiosities. This miscellany will appeal to everyone – not just to the interested Mind, Body, Spirit beginner but also to the profound sceptic and, equally, to those who are well-read and highly experienced in the area.

I have been fascinated by the various fields of Mind, Body, Spirit since childhood. We were a family of seekers, enchanted by the esoteric, intrigued by the arcane. I was being pulled into yoga asanas before I went to school and was reading the Tarot by the time I was seven. I grew up surrounded by books on Kabbalah and Zen Buddhism, listening to Sufi poetry and Chinese Cheng music. My mother was a homeopath; and as a teenager I investigated herbalism, flower remedies and aromatherapy. I later trained in past life therapy, SHEN energy healing, shamanism, and Jungian art and dream therapy. As a journalist, I have dedicated the last twenty years to investigating the MBS world and

I have written over twenty books on the subject. I'll be honest, I didn't think that it could hold too many more surprises for me.

However, I will freely admit that writing this book has been a journey of near-constant revelation and delight. I realized that, however much you may think you know, there is always more to discover. For example, in the course of researching this book, I learnt that myomancy is divination by observing the movement and behaviour of mice (so a visit to the pet shop might be in order!), and I can now differentiate between the two major types of ghost in the Viking sagas. I was intrigued to find that the Jewish menorah symbolized the Kabbalistic Tree of Life and, to my utter amazement, I discovered that people were reading about (and recording pictures of) crop circles way back in 1678. I am now itching to read a plethora of further unfamiliar esoteric texts and I have an overwhelming urge to visit a host of sacred sites all over the world.

In short, I have become absorbed and entranced, captivated and enlightened during the creation of this book. My sincere hope is that you will gain every bit as much from reading it as I have from writing it.

Jane Alexander

• THE THREE TYPES OF KARMA •

A fundamental concept of Eastern (Hindu, Buddhist, Jain, Sikh) thought, karma is the law of moral consequences. In literal terms, if you do something bad, you will, at some point, pay for it; if you do something good, you will receive kindness and happiness in return. More profoundly, every thought, word and deed is weighed on the scales of an eternal justice. Even if you have been virtuous in this life, misfortune and sickness can come from the accumulated bad karma of past lives. Until you pay off your "karmic debts", and expunge your karma, you are condemned to repeat life again and again, through reincarnation. Three types of karma are described in Hindu texts:

Sanchita *(accumulated works):* All the accumulated karma of past incarnations, this is responsible for the body that each person has in their current life, as well as the situation in which they find themselves. This karma is destroyed when knowledge of Brahman, the Eternal, is attained. It can be modified by good deeds and pure thoughts.

Prarabdha *(fructifying works):* Selected from the *Sanchita* karma, this type of karma influences a person's life in their present incarnation. It cannot be avoided or changed.

Kriyamana or Agami or Vartamana *(current works):* This is the karma that is being created for the future: the way our thoughts and actions in this life will affect our future life and incarnations. This karma can be altered by correct attitude, as well as by particular rites.

••• ❖ •••

••• THE BIRTH OF MODERN ••• AROMATHERAPY

Essential oils have been used therapeutically and cosmetically for thousands of years – in Egypt, Babylon, China and India. Babylonian clay tablets from c.1800BCE record the purchase of cedar, myrrh and cypress oils. However, aromatherapy as we know it today originated in the early 20th century when French chemist **René-Maurice Gattefossé** (1881–1950) was working in his family's perfume laboratory. One day in 1910, having burned his hand in a lab accident, he immersed it in lavender oil (the nearest available liquid) to gain relief. He was intrigued to notice that the pain lessened much more quickly than normal and that the wound started to heal the next day, without blistering or scarring. This observation caused him to turn his attention, and research, to the healing properties of essential oils, including exploration of their antiseptic properties in military hospitals during World War I.

His renowned book *Aromathérapie: Les Huiles Essentielles Hormones Végétales* was published in 1937. The first book on the healing qualities of oils, this was translated into English as *Gattefossé's Aromatherapy*, and is still in print today.

• THEORIES ABOUT STONEHENGE •

Current estimates suggest that Stonehenge was built in stages between c.3100 and c.1930BCE. However, even today there is no overall consensus about the monument's original purpose.

Heroic burial site

Geoffrey of Monmouth's *Historia Regum Britanniae* (History of the Kings of Britain), written in the 1130s, claimed that Stonehenge was constructed as a burial place for fallen British heroes by King Ambrosius, uncle of King Arthur. The magician Merlin is described as using his arts to transport the monument ready-made from a hilltop in Ireland.

Roman temple

Commissioned by James I to survey Stonehenge, the 17th-century architect Inigo Jones concluded that of all Britain's early inhabitants, only the Romans had the resources to build the monument, which he thought was a temple to the sky god Coelus.

The Druid connection

In the mid-17th century, antiquary John Aubrey identified an outer ring of small, man-made cavities, filled with rubble, which are still known today as the Aubrey holes. In his posthumously published *Monumenta Britannica*, he claimed the monument was a pagan temple built by the Druids. William Stukeley expressed a similar theory in 1740, but believed that the Druids followed in the tradition of the Christian patriarchs.

Astronomical calendar

Sir Joseph Norman Lockyer, discoverer of helium and founder of the journal *Nature*, argued in 1906 that the stones marked crucial points in the cyclical movements of the sun, moon and stars. This theory was amplified in the 1960s by Gerald S. Hawkins, who used computer technology to conclude that the monument was aligned to predict lunar eclipses. In the next decade, a retired Oxford professor, Alexander Thom, used surveying equipment to make the case that it was the centre of a complex of megalithic sites, which had jointly served as an immense prehistoric astronomical observatory.

Focus for psychic energy

Alfred Watkins's pioneering study of ley lines, *The Old Straight Track* (1925), identified Stonehenge as a nexus point where two principal lines meet. In Watkins' wake, investigators have used all sorts of techniques, from dowsing to geomancy, to try to establish the existence of spiritual force-fields at the site. Ufologists have claimed sightings of unidentified flying objects in the skies above the monument.

Prehistoric burial site

Recent archaeological work by the Stonehenge Riverside Project has suggested that the monument was indeed a burial site, as Geoffrey of Monmouth originally proposed. In the modern view, however, the burials date back as far as 3000BCE and continued for at least the first 500 years of the site's existence.

• CELEBRATED PREMONITIONS •

Pharaoh Tuthmose IV,
Egypt, 14th century BCE
In a dream, young prince Tuthmose was told by the Sphinx of Giza statue (which was over 1,000 years old and chin-high in sand) that he would one day rule Egypt – even though he had elder brothers with better claims to the throne. In return, the Sphinx asked to be restored to its former glory. On waking, the prince sent workmen to clear away the sand. He later became pharaoh as predicted. (This account is told in a stele unearthed between the Sphinx's paws in 1818.)

Emperor Motecuhzoma,
Mexico, 1519
A legend of the Spanish conquest of Mexico tells that Papantzin, recently deceased sister of Aztec emperor Motecuhzoma, came to him in a dream four days after her burial to warn of the approach of ships that posed a threat to his realm. Within months, Hernán Cortés and his Spanish conquistadors arrived, imprisoned Motecuhzoma and took over his kingdom.

Robert Morris, USA,
18th century
Tobacco planter Robert Morris was inclined to call off a warship inspection after dreaming he would be killed by one of its cannons. The commander promised that no cannons would be fired, so Morris toured the ship. As he was being rowed to shore, the captain raised his hand to brush a fly from his face. Mistaking this as a command to fire, a gunner discharged his cannon, and Morris was killed by shrapnel, as he had foreseen.

Lord Lyttelton, London, 1779
A 35-year-old English nobleman, Lord Lyttelton, was awoken one night by the spectre of a woman in white who warned him he would be dead within three days. On the third day, Lord Lyttelton was still in good health, and in high spirits at dinner. But just before midnight, as he was getting ready for bed, he suffered a seizure, and never recovered.

Abraham Lincoln,
Washington, D.C., 1865
President Lincoln told aides that he had dreamed of himself wandering through the White House in mourning – in a deathly silence broken only by subdued sobbing. Reaching the East Room, he saw a corpse lying on a catafalque guarded by soldiers, one of whom informed a bystander that the body was that of the president, killed by an assassin. Three days later, Lincoln was fatally shot by John Wilkes Booth as he watched a play in Ford's Theatre, Washington, D.C..

Morgan Robertson, USA, 1898
American writer Morgan Robertson penned a novel entitled *Futility* 14 years before the *Titanic* sank. In the novel, a luxury British liner sails across the North Atlantic on its maiden voyage, smashes into a huge iceberg and sinks, causing the loss of hundreds of lives, their number swollen by a shortage of lifeboats. Most remarkable of all was the name he chose to give the ship – the *Titan*.

• • • DIY ART THERAPY • • •

Painting, drawing and other forms of artistic expression are often used by art therapists to unlock psychological trauma in patients, and to help with overall emotional and mental well-being. Art can also be used as *self*-therapy. All you need is a selection of pens, crayons and paints, a few paintbrushes, several large sheets of paper and some privacy.

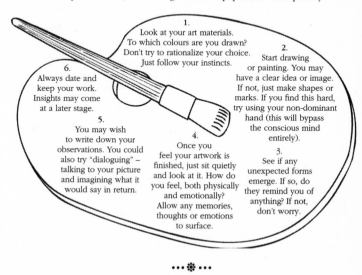

1. Look at your art materials. To which colours are you drawn? Don't try to rationalize your choice. Just follow your instincts.

2. Start drawing or painting. You may have a clear idea or image. If not, just make shapes or marks. If you find this hard, try using your non-dominant hand (this will bypass the conscious mind entirely).

3. See if any unexpected forms emerge. If so, do they remind you of anything? If not, don't worry.

4. Once you feel your artwork is finished, just sit quietly and look at it. How do you feel, both physically and emotionally? Allow any memories, thoughts or emotions to surface.

5. You may wish to write down your observations. You could also try "dialoguing" – talking to your picture and imagining what it would say in return.

6. Always date and keep your work. Insights may come at a later stage.

• REBIRTHING: WHAT HAPPENS? •

Rebirthing uses "conscious connected breathing" (a controlled form of hyperventilation) to explore unconsciously held emotions and assumptions. The theory is that by breathing continuously, without a pause between inhalation and exhalation, you change the levels of carbon dioxide in the brain. You then enter a light, self-induced trance, during which repressed emotions and memories can surface and be recognized and discussed. Rebirthers believe that this breathing technique also builds up *qi* or *chi* (life energy), which can help to free inner blockages.

Sessions with a qualified practitioner usually last 2–3 hours. Initially, you spend time exploring your issues with the rebirther. Then you lie on the floor with your eyes shut as the rebirther guides you through the required breathing technique for 60–75 minutes. It's not uncommon to suffer temporary side-effects, such as cramping or paralysis (tetany). During the last part of the session, your rebirther will help you to integrate into your conscious, daily life the material that has emerged.

Caution: Never try this without qualified, expert guidance.

✠═✳═✠

• • • I CHING BASICS • • •

The *I Ching*, or *Book of Changes*, may be the oldest book in the world (1122–770BCE). Certainly, it records the oldest known form of divination, going back 5,000 years. The *I Ching* teaches that the universe is an infinite void, *tai chi*, and that all objects within it owe their individuality to a combination of yin (negative polarity) and yang (positive polarity).

Using the *I Ching* for life guidance involves defining a question and then throwing coins (more traditionally, yarrow sticks) to yield an answer in the form of sets of broken (yin) and unbroken (yang) lines. The arrangement of these lines is determined by the sides on which the coins land: three heads, or two heads and one tails, yield a continuous line; three tails, or two tails and one heads, a broken line. An arrangement of six stacked lines makes a hexagram; three stacked lines form a trigram.

Once one of the 64 possible hexagram permutations has been shown, the *I Ching* is consulted for its meaning. Some hexagrams include "moving lines" – prompted by three heads or three tails: these are lines with a changed pattern. When this occurs, the original hexagram is consulted alongside the transformed version.

••• ✿ •••

• • • THE I CHING TRIGRAMS • • •

Each of the 64 *I Ching* hexagrams is made up of two out of eight possible trigrams. The upper trigram in a hexagram is traditionally associated with the outer aspects of a situation, the lower trigram with the inner aspects. Working with trigrams is a good introduction to the fuller version of the *I Ching*, using hexagrams. Moving lines (see above) are ignored.

NAME	TRIGRAM	TITLE	HEALTH	ANIMALS	PROPERTIES
Ch'ien		Heaven	Head, mind	Dragon	Creative, active, light
K'un		Earth	Blood, reproductive system	Cow, mare	Receptive, passive, dark
Chen		Thunder	Birth, feet	Horse	Arousing, moving
K'an		Water	Anxiety, ears, heart	Boar, pig	Abysmal, dangerous
Ken		Mountain	Swellings, obstruction, fingers	Rat, watchdog, black-billed bird	Still, stubborn
Sun		Wind	Breath, thighs	None	Gentle, penetrating
Li		Fire	Eyes	Pheasant, phoenix	Clinging, beautiful
Tui		Lake	Mouth, tongue	Sheep	Joyous, pleasurable

• • • *MYTHS OF HUMAN ORIGIN* • • •

Each mythology has its own beliefs about the origins of humanity. Some creation myths describe a process of trial and error. In others the first people came from Mother Earth or from plants (for example, as seeds).

Norse/Germanic: Frost-giants (born of a primeval giant, Ymir) existed before the gods, who annihilated these giants, created dwarves to hold up the sky, and then created the first man and woman – from two tree trunks.

Greek: Cronus, king of the Titan gods, was defeated by a new race of gods, the Olympians, led by the great Zeus, Cronus's son. In one tale the first humans were clay figures made by the Titan Prometheus, who received this privilege from Zeus as thanks for support in the war; in another, there was a succession of human races (*see p15*), created by Cronus and Zeus in turn.

Tibetan: The Epic of Gesar claims that the six clans of ancient Tibet emerged from birds' eggs that were broken open by divine blacksmiths under orders from the gods.

North American Indian: The Hopi believe that their ancestors were led from the underworld to their home in the American Southwest by their divine creator, Spider Woman, who taught them survival skills.

Australian Aboriginal: The primordial deity, the Rainbow Snake, swallowed the first people, then regurgitated them to populate the land.

• *ESSENTIAL OILS THAT PESTS HATE* •

Some essential oils can help to deter common household pests. Add a small amount of your chosen oil to water and spray the resulting mixture around the house or garden; or drop the oil onto strips of paper or cotton-wool balls, and place them around windows and doors.

Ants .... peppermint
Aphids .... hyssop, peppermint, spearmint
Fleas .... lavender, lemongrass, peppermint
Flies .... lavender
Gnats .... patchouli, spearmint
Lice .... cedarwood, spearmint
Mice .... peppermint, spearmint
Mosquitoes .... lavender, peppermint
Moths .... camphor, cedarwood, lemon, lemongrass
Slugs .... cedarwood, hyssop, pine
Spiders .... pennyroyal*
Ticks .... lavender, sage, thyme

* **Caution:** Keep away from children and pets.

• • • *IMPORTANT SUN SYMBOLS* • • •

The sun, source of all life, was naturally enough a key symbol of antiquity. It was generally seen as a masculine, active energy, while the moon was feminine and passive, although in a few myth systems the sun was a goddess (the Japanese Amaterasu, the Norse Sol). The examples below indicate the range of solar symbolism around the globe.

The Buddhist parasol or sunshade: Tibetan dignitaries were shielded from the sun by elaborate parasols, which came to symbolize the majesty of Buddhas and bodhisattvas. Further implied was the idea of shielding oneself from destructive emotion. The sunshade also symbolized the sun itself: the spokes as the rays, the shaft as the world-axis.

The winged sun disk: Ancient Egyptians used this to symbolize the power and majesty of the sun god Ra, creator of the world and ruler of the skies, who was also known as the Son of Righteousness, with healing in his wings.

The chariot of the sun: This symbol is found in several mythologies. In the Norse *Edda*, the chariot was pulled by two horses, Arvak and Alsvid, and driven by the goddess Sól; in Greek myth, the sun chariot was driven by the god Apollo; and there are similar versions in Persian (Mithras) and Phrygian (Attis) myth.

Obelisk: In ancient Egypt, this symbol represented the sun god Ra. The tip of a stone obelisk would often be covered with shining metal to reflect the first rays of the sun. During the reign of the pharaoh Akhenaten, an obelisk was said to be a petrified ray of the life-giving force of the sun, Aten.

Sun wheels, or sun crosses: Prehistoric petroglyphs (rock carvings) of a cross surrounded by a circle are reminiscent of a wheel – yet were engraved long before the wheel's invention. Found as far afield as Scotland, Spain, Mesopotamia and the Indus valley, they are thought to represent the sun, its diurnal and annual passage, and its generative power.

Swastika: Although indelibly linked with Germany's Nazi past, this ancient and auspicious Hindu symbol traditionally signifies the sun and the sun god Surya. Its four arms represent the four directions, the four Vedas (Sanskrit sacred texts), the stages of life from birth to death, and the four seasons.

• THE FIVE AGES OF HUMANKIND •

The notion of a bygone golden age, when people lived happier lives, goes back at least as far as the 7th-century-BCE Greek poet Hesiod. In his *Works and Days* he presented a view of the successive ages of humankind, culminating in Hesiod's own time, the Age of Iron:

Golden Age
Under the rule of Zeus's father, the Titan Cronus, people enjoyed lives of comfort and ease, without the miseries of old age. Death came to them like sleep. Eventually they were wiped out by an earthquake or a flood.

↓

Silver Age
Ruled by Zeus, people worked for a living and built houses for shelter. They enjoyed an extended childhood, but then did harm to each other and neglected the gods. Zeus annihilated them for their bad behaviour.

↓

Bronze Age
In this age people made weapons and tools of bronze and waged perpetual war. Their houses were bronze, too. Their violent lifestyle eventually led to their downfall. They ended up forgotten, in Hades.

↓

Heroic Age
Peopled by demi-gods with human mothers. Among them were the heroes of the Theban and Trojan wars. Many fell in battle. Some found a posthumous home in the Isles of the Blessed.

↓

Age of Iron
This race was born to toil. Families fell apart and evil triumphed. Hesiod believed it would end when babies were born white-haired.

••• ❁ •••

• •THE SEVEN TYPES OF PRAYER • •

Some theologians argue that prayer can be divided simply into two categories – in everyday terms, those that say "please" and those that say "thank you". Others, however, identify seven basic prayer types:

Petition: Seeking divine aid
Confession: Owning up to sins and asking for forgiveness
Adoration: Praise for, and love of, God
Intercession: Praying on behalf of other people
Meditation/contemplation: Silence in the presence of God
Thanksgiving: Gratitude for all our blessings
Consecration: Surrendering one's life to the will and service of God

• SOME UNUSUAL KINDS OF MASSAGE •

Biodynamic massage: Often a deep massage, although there are gentle, flowing movements too. Devised in the 1960s by the Norwegian Gerda Boyessen. The therapist pays particular attention to noises made from the gut (psychoperistalsis). The principal aim is psychological release. The subject decides whether to take off any clothing.

Chavutti thirumal: The Indian "rope massage". The subject lies on a mat unclothed, except for a towel between the legs. The therapist uses his or her feet to give a deep, flowing massage, using an overhead rope to balance.

Chua ka: An ancient Mongolian form of massage, traditionally given to remove a warrior's fear before battle. Adopted in the 1960s by Oscar Ichazo, it is now performed to eliminate patterns of held tension, using long, fluid strokes to probe into deep tissue. Also renowned for its "instant face-lift" effect when done on the face. You wear only underpants but are well covered with towels.

Hawaiian (huna) massage: With smooth, repetitive movements over the whole body, this massage aims to harmonize mind, body and soul, as well as reconnect the subject with the world's beauty. Scented oils are used. The therapist uses the whole length of the forearm for some moves. The subject wears a special loincloth and lies on a massage table in a very hot room.

Thai massage: Often called "lazy man's yoga" or "passive yoga", because the therapist will safely stretch and bend you into positions you could never reach on your own. He or she also uses hands, feet and elbows to free the flow of *qi* (vital energy). Performed on a mat on the floor, wearing loose clothing.

Tibetan massage: A gentle yet powerful massage with spiced oils (often ginger and cardamom). It aims to free energy blockages via acupressure points. The subject wears only underpants but is well covered with towels.

Trager®: Developed by acrobat and boxer Milton Trager in Miami, Florida, in the 1930s, this very gentle form of bodywork is supremely soothing to the central nervous system and also helps with neuromuscular problems. Performed on a couch, the subject wearing underwear or loose clothing.

Tui na: A Chinese massage that uses acupressure to bring the body back into balance. It is an intense treatment, stringent and down-to-earth rather than instantly feel-good. Particularly effective for neck, shoulder and back pain. The subject remains fully clothed, on a couch, on the floor or seated in a chair.

Watsu: Massage and manipulation techniques are carried out as you float (in swimwear) in a warm pool of water, cradled by the therapist. Releases stress and muscle tension, and taps into and releases psychological trauma. Related techniques are: Water Dance and Jehara Technique.

• DREAM KEYS TO HEALTH •

Experts believe that dreams can give vital insights into our physical well-being. The unconscious, the source of dreams, understands our bodies as well as our desires and fears far better than our rational minds do.

A house on fire can warn of high blood pressure or that you are "burnt out".

An engine leaking oil can be a sign of low energy or anaemia.

 A black dog can hint at depression.

Clocks symbolize the human heart and worries about time (biological clock, mortality). The ticking is linked to the heartbeat. A clock going too fast could mean that you are overworking your body.

Stairs that are rickety or falling down can indicate problems with or weakness in the spine.

A purse or handbag can indicate female genitals or the womb (as well as feelings of self-worth). An empty purse can therefore suggest fertility worries, or sexual unfulfilment.

Anything soggy, mouldy or steaming (such as steaming hay or a mouldy kitchen) can indicate candida overgrowth.

A knife can suggest a fear of – and aversion to – intimacy, ambivalence about sex, or anxieties about surgery.

Frogs, fish, eggs, acorns and circular pools can all be indicators of early pregnancy.

••• ❖ •••

• SUNNI AND SHI'ITE MUSLIMS •

Modern Islam is broadly divided into two main branches: Sunnism and Shi'ism. Many Muslims regard these as completely separate faiths, rather than subdivisions of the same religion. Sunnis constitute the vast majority of Muslims (85%), while Shi'ites (in Iran and Iraq) make up just 15%.

The split between Sunnis and Shi'ites can be traced back to 632CE, the year of the Prophet Mohammed's death. A debate ensued over who was his rightful successor as leader, or "caliph", of the Muslim community – Abu Bakr, Mohammed's close companion and an early convert to Islam (supported by the Sunnis), or Ali ibn Abi Talib, Mohammed's cousin and son-in-law (supported by the Shi'ites).

Both groups agree on the principles of the Five Pillars of Islam (*see p46*). However, Shi'ites believe in a leadership of imams – bearers of the light of Mohammed and religiously inspired leaders of the community. Mecca and Medina are the holiest sites for both Sunnis and Shi'ites, but the tombs of the imams are also important for Shi'ites (*see also p93*).

⊹━✳━⊹

⋅⋅ PSYCHOLOGICAL SYMBOLISM ⋅⋅
OF THE GRAIL QUEST

The Grail legends, best known from the story of King Arthur, first emerged in the early 12th century. Modern readings derive mainly from Chrétien de Troyes's *Le Contes du Graal* and Wolfram von Eschenbach's *Parzival*. Rich in cross-cultural symbolism and psychological insight, the saga can be seen as a paradigm for the realization of self.

Parsifal *(Perceval)*
The fool in the Tarot *(see p131)*; the self on the journey of life.

The Round Table
Social harmony; equality and unity.

The Grail
The female, the divine feminine, the womb; spiritual destiny; rebirth, reincarnation; the anima.

The Grail King/ Rich Fisher
Spiritual sickness, meaninglessness; wrongly directed life energy; emergence of individuality from the sea of the unconscious.

The Sword
Discrimination and judgment; power and responsibility; victory in battle; the animus.

The Lance
The spear of Longinus (Roman soldier whose spear pierced Christ's side); male energy.

The Red Knight
The shadow self; raw, physical, primitive emotion.

The Wasteland
Stagnation of the soul; misdirection of the psyche.

••• ✿ •••

• • • OM • • •

The mantra *Om* is sacred to Hindus, Sikhs, Jains and Buddhists. The *Mandukya Upanishad* describes it as " the eternal word ... what was, what is, what shall be, and what is in eternity".

Yoga philosophy teaches that chanting *Om* will unite you with the cosmos. The mantra is made up of three separate sounds: "aaa", "uuu" and "mmm". In Vedic chanting, it is given four counts: three counts for the "aaauuu" (a combination of "a" and "u"), a half-count for the "mmm" and a half-count of silence.

Om is also called the *mula mantra*, meaning "root mantra": it is often chanted before other mantras, and before and after a reading from the Vedas.

The visual elements of the Sanskrit symbol represent the four states of consciousness (1–4), and the world of illusion (5):

1. Waking *(jagrat)*
2. Dreaming *(swapna)*
3. Deep sleep *(sushupti)*
4. Transcendental state *(turiya)*
5. World of illusion *(maya)* that veils true awareness

. . FAMOUS ENCOUNTERS . .
WITH THE PARANORMAL

What? The Tedworth Drummer
Where & when? Tedworth (now North Tidworth), Wiltshire, England, 1660s

A magistrate, John Mompesson, confiscated the drum of a noisy itinerant musician. He was then plagued by crashes and moving objects caused by an apparition in his children's bedroom, until the drummer, sentenced to transportation for theft, was finally shipped overseas.

What? The Bell Witch
Where & when? Robertson County, Tennessee, USA, 1817–1821

The house of prosperous cotton farmer John Bell, where he lived with his wife and nine children, was plagued by violent noises. The children were scratched and had their hair pulled, and the ghost talked through one of the daughters, using her as a medium. The spirit was sometimes benevolent: it rescued one of the boys from quicksand, and also dropped fruit out of thin air, into the laps of visitors. But when old John Bell died, he was found to have been poisoned. The ghost was heard singing and shrieking with joy at the funeral.

What? The Amherst Poltergeist
Where & when? Amherst, Nova Scotia, Canada, 1878

The boyfriend of a teenage girl, Esther Cox, made an unsuccessful attempt to rape her at gunpoint and then fled the neighbourhood, never to be seen again. A week later, objects started moving of their own accord, loud crashes were heard, and at one point Esther's skin became red, hot and swollen. In a doctor's presence, a pillow flew from under her head and hovered in mid-air, the blankets flew off the bed, and writing appeared on the wall, stating: "Esther Cox, you are mine to kill."

What? The Winchester Mystery Mansion
Where & when? San Jose, California, USA, 1880s onward

Widowed heiress to the Winchester rifle fortune, Sarah Winchester believed that her family had been cursed by the spirits of people killed by the weapons made in her husband's factory. She communed with these spirits and claimed that it was they who provided her with the guidelines for an eccentric sprawling mansion, which was built continuously between 1884 and 1922, with staircases leading to nowhere and doors that open onto sheer drops.

What? The Most Haunted House in England
Where & when? Borley Rectory, England, 1930s

Built in 1863 on the site of a former monastery, the rectory acquired a reputation for unexplained footsteps, strange knockings and the appearance of a ghostly nun. When a new vicar moved in, in 1928, celebrated ghost hunter Harry Price was sent to investigate. He reported keys flying out of locks, floating bricks, and a glass candlestick plunging down a staircase. He rented the rectory for a year, and wrote two books about it. Fakery has been suspected.

The mystique of secret and subversive societies, especially those with religious or occult roots, has led to a proliferation of conspiracy theories. For example, the Templars were thought to have been secret guardians of the Ark of the Covenant or the Holy Grail.

Freemasons: Inspired by the Temple of Solomon, the square and compass of the regalia being the tools of the masons (builders) of that temple. The first Great Lodge of England was founded in 1717. In the 18th century, their progressive ideas led to condemnation by the Catholic Church. Masons pass initiations to achieve three degrees of membership: Apprentice, Fellow or Journeyman, and Master Mason. Mainly known for charitable work and social networking.

Illuminati: Founded in 1776 by Adam Weishaupt, a professor at the University of Ingolstadt, Bavaria. Served as a cover for the spread of Enlightenment ideas, bringing together leading freethinkers and intellectuals (Goethe, Herder) at a time of government nervousness. Secret societies were banned in Bavaria in 1784, and the group broke up.

Knights Templar: The Poor Fellow-Soldiers of Christ and of the Temple of Solomon. A military, crusading order, powerful in the Middle Ages. Endorsed by the Church c.1129. They created an economic network, with an early banking system, and built forts in Europe and the Holy Land. Templar knights wore white mantles with a red cross. Rumours about initiation rites caused mistrust. In 1307, many members in France were burned at the stake. The Pope dissolved the Order in 1312.

Rosicrucians: Also known as the Brethren of the Rose Cross. A secret society of mystics, with origins in medieval Germany. Behind it was the mysterious figure of Christian Rosenkreuz (thought by some to be a pseudonym of Francis Bacon). They believed in occult wisdom within an ascetic lifestyle. The Rosicrucian manifestos, dating from the early 17th century, are a cryptic mixture of parable, Kabbalism and alchemy, including the notion of the "chymical marriage". Egyptian and druidic elements were later added. The ultimate goal was the universal reformation of humankind.

Order of the Golden Dawn: Founded by MacGregor Mathers, a former Freemason, along with two associates, in 1887. The group had three membership orders, with twelve grades, from neophytes to the topmost ranks of magus and ipsissimus. The movement flourished in the 1890s, attracting well-known figures such as W.B. Yeats and Aleister Crowley. Members met in the Isis-Urania Temple, London, to practise rituals outlined in coded documents, the Cipher manuscripts. The group was torn apart by schisms. One section remained loyal to Mathers, who renamed his branch Alpha et Omega; another, retaining the original title, abandoned magic for Christian mysticism.

• TIMES OF ISLAMIC PRAYER •

Islam requires that all fit and able Muslims pray at least five times every day, each time facing toward the Kaaba, the sacred shrine at the heart of the holy city of Mecca (*see p93*), in Saudi Arabia:

> *Dawn prayer (Salat al-Fajr)*
> *Midday prayer (Salat al-Dhuhr)*
> *Afternoon prayer (Salat al-Asr)*
> *Dusk prayer (Salat al-Maghrib)*
> *Night prayer (Salat al-Isha'a)*

••• ✿ •••

• HUMMING BEES, SHINING SKULLS: • TWO BREATHING EXERCISES

Pranayama are yogic exercises used to direct subtle energy, or *prana* (*see p104*), to boost well-being and, ultimately, to help us to reach higher states of consciousness. Here are two traditional *pranayama* practices:

Brahmari: humming-bee breath

A relaxing, cheering exercise that encourages focus on the out-breath. It warms up the vocal cords, and strengthens and sweetens the voice.

1. Sit with your back straight, close your eyes and inhale through your nose.

2. Exhale, and start to hum (through the nose). Sense the vibrations of the humming and gradually shift them around your lips, mouth, head and chest. Vary your pitch until you find a sound that you can sustain smoothly and comfortably.

3. When you naturally come to the end of your humming exhalation, fully inhale. Then start to hum again on the next exhalation. Once you complete this, you have done one round. Practise five to ten rounds to feel the positive effects.

Kapalabhati: shining-skull breath

Has an energizing, clarifying effect. Do it any time you need a boost – stop if you feel uncomfortable or short of breath.

1. Sit with your back straight. Lift your right hand, palm down, and place your fingers below your nostrils, pointing left. Close your eyes. Inhale through your nose.

2. Contract your abdominal muscles to exhale sharply through your nose. Imagine you are blowing out a candle using your nose, feeling the air on your hand. Do this four times in all. Resume normal breathing.

3. Repeat the whole exercise three times. You may notice an exhilarating, "shining" feeling around the top of your forehead.

Caution: Avoid if you have poor lung capacity, high/low blood pressure or suffer from ear complaints.

··· *LEGENDARY PLACES* ···
IN CELTIC MYTH

Lyonesse: In Arthurian legend, the birthplace of Tristan. Later identified with Cornish tales of a sunken kingdom off the Scilly Isles.

Annwn: The Otherworld described in Welsh myth, a place of eternal youth, where disease did not exist and food was always abundant. Ruled by Arawn.

Camelot: Site of Arthur's court, with its Round Table, according to late myths (early tales place the court at Caerleon, S. Wales). Possible sites include Winchester, Cadbury (Somerset) and Camelford (Cornwall).

Tir na Nog: The Land of Eternal Youth in Irish legend, said to be the home of the Tuatha de Danaan, mythical early inhabitants of Ireland who became associated with the fairy folk and also with the pagan gods of the Celtic world. Often associated with the Isles of the Blessed.

Ys: Breton equivalent of Lyonnesse. Protected from high tides by a dyke, with a gate to allow boats in at low tide, it was flooded when the Devil, disguised as a handsome knight, persuaded the king's daughter to give him the key to the gate, then opened it during a storm.

Avalon: In legend, the island where Arthur's sword Excalibur was forged and where the king was taken, mortally wounded, after his last battle at Camlann. The name may mean "The Isle of Apples". Often associated with Glastonbury Tor, which was once surrounded by marshland.

··· ❀ ···

··· *POPULAR CHINESE* ···
MEDICINE INGREDIENTS

Developed over thousands of years, Chinese medicine operates on the assumption that all processes within the human body interrelate not only with each other but also with the wider natural environment. The following ingredients – sourced from plants and animals – are traditionally valued for their healing properties:

Peach stone (to improve blood circulation)
Bear's gall (to relieve pain)
Seahorse* (for respiratory problems)
Rhinoceros horn* (to ease fever and convulsions)
Tiger bone* (to treat arthritis)
Honeysuckle flower (to reduce toxins)
Bletilla tuber (to stop bleeding)
Tangerine peel (to regulate *qi*)

*These species are endangered, so purchasing these ingredients is strictly illegal.

• FREUD'S FAMOUS CASE STUDIES •

Sigmund Freud based many of his theories about the workings of the unconscious (the Oedipus complex, infantile sexuality, repression, sublimation, transference) on work with particular patients. In his published case studies he used pseudonyms to protect identities.

"Anna O."
Real name: Bertha Pappenheim, Austrian-Jewish feminist, aged 21
Recorded in: *Studies in Hysteria (1895)*
A patient, initially, of Josef Breuer, with whom Freud collaborated. Symptoms included hallucinations of skulls, a severe cough, a paralyzed arm and an inability to drink water. Interpreted as suppressed grief at her father's life-threatening illness. She redirected her sexual fantasies to Breuer (transference), imagining she was pregnant by him.

"Dora"
Real name: Ida Bauer, daughter of a wealthy Austrian textile industrialist, aged 18
Recorded in: *Fragments of an Analysis of a Case of Hysteria (1905)*
Freud's longest case study on a woman. She suffered from depression and hysteria, and dreamed about a burning house containing her mother's jewel case, which her father would not let her rescue. He was having an affair with a family friend, whose husband had made advances toward Dora when she was around 14. Interpreted as repressed sexual feelings toward both this man and her father.

"The Rat Man"
Real name: believed to be Ernst Lanzer, Austrian lawyer, aged 29
Recorded in: *Notes Upon A Case of Obsessional Neurosis (1909)*
Not actually a patient of Freud's: analyzed from the literature. Obsessed by a fantasy of his fiancée and deceased father being forced to undergo a military torture involving rats being suspended beneath them so that they gnawed into the anus. Interpreted as a mix of love and aggression felt for these two people, as well as repressed homosexual desires.

"Little Hans"
Real name: Herbert Graf (later a renowned Austrian-American opera producer), aged 5
Recorded in: *Analysis of a Phobia in a Five-year-old Boy (1909)*
Developed a fear of horses after witnessing, aged 4, a heavily laden horse collapsing on a bystander, leading to the death of both. Interpreted as incestuous desires for his mother, castration anxiety, jealous fear of his father (Oedipus complex).

"The Wolf Man"
Real name: Sergei Konstantinovitch Pankejeff, Russian aristocrat, aged 23
Recorded in: *The History of an Infantile Neurosis (1918)*
Suffered from anxiety and depression. Haunted by a childhood dream in which white wolves sat on branches and stared at him through a window. Interpreted as a repressed memory of his parents having sex in the same room when he was a baby, thinking him asleep.

• • • THE SEVEN CHAKRAS • • •

Yogic tradition teaches that we have two bodies – our tangible, physical body and our "subtle", or energetic, body. Seven subtle energy centres, or *chakras* (meaning "wheels" in Sanskrit), lie along the midline of the subtle body, within the spine, at the points where the main *nadis* (energy channels) intersect (*see p104*). The chart below shows how each chakra is associated with not only a particular part of the body but also a particular colour, mantra, and mental or emotional benefit.

Meditation on the chakras can help to release physical and emotional tensions connected to their individual location. To meditate on a particular chakra, visualize it as a radiant lotus in the relevant place within your body, or as a spinning wheel of light – in that chakra's colour. Breathe in and imagine energy flowing into the chakra; then breathe out and imagine that same energy radiating throughout your body. Gently repeat the seed mantra of your chosen chakra to enhance the benefits (pronunciation of the Sanskrit terms is shown in brackets).

CHAKRA NAME	LOCATION	COLOUR	SEED MANTRA	MEDITATION BENEFIT
Sahasrara	Crown of the head	White or golden	Om (*aaa-uuu-mmm*)	Liberation of the mind
Ajna	Centre of the forehead, the "third eye"	Deep blue or violet	Om (*aaa-uuu-mmm*)	Enhanced intuition
Vishuddha	Throat	Sky blue	Ham (*hanng*)	Improved communication
Anahata	Centre of chest	Green	Yam (*yanng*)	Spiritual and emotional opening
Manipura	Solar plexus	Yellow	Ram (*ranng*)	Transcendence of physical desire
Swadhisthana	Around the sacrum	Orange	Vam (*vonng*)	Emotional balance and enhanced creativity
Muladhara	Perineum, between the anus and genitals	Red	Lam (*lonng*)	Release of deeply held anxiety

• • • THE ORIGINS OF TAI CHI • • •

The roots of this tradition are mysterious, but it seems that Taoist martial arts were being practised well over 2,000 years ago. Legend has it that the Indian monk Bodhidharma taught the monks of the Shaolin temple a form of Zen boxing in the 5th century – to develop discipline, strength, flexibility and self-defence. However, the origins of modern *tai chi* lie in the 14th century, with the Taoist monk Chang San Feng. He is said to have either observed or dreamed about (texts disagree) a fight between a bird and a snake, where the snake's suppleness and grace won over the bird's fierce pecking and clawing. This inspired him to develop a martial art that relied on yielding rather than aggression, softness rather than hardness.

Over time, the body movements he devised evolved, with several different lineages emerging. There is now a huge number of tai chi variations but the most commonly taught in the West include Yang (long and short forms), Wu, Sun, Chen and Wudang.

••• ✿ •••

• FAMOUS ORACLES •

Delphic Oracle
• At the Temple of Delphi on Mt Parnassus, in ancient Greece.
• The god Apollo spoke through the prophetess Pythia.
• Her enigmatic prophecies were interpreted by the temple priests.
• Statesmen often consulted the oracle before important decisions.

Nechung
• A role originally performed in the Nechung Monastery outside Lhasa, Tibet.
• As the state oracle of Tibet, this man was consulted by the Dalai Lamas before important decisions.
• He reportedly predicted the current Dalai Lama's flight from Tibet in 1959 before accompanying him on the journey to Dharamsala, India.

Cumaean Sibyl
• The priestess residing over the Apollonian oracle at Cumae, near Naples, in southern Italy.
• The most famous sibyl (prophetess) of ancient Rome.

• *The Sibylline Books*, a collection of prophecies consulted by Rome's rulers in times of crisis, may have contained some of her pronouncements.

Dodona
• A shrine in NW Greece.
• Dedicated to the Mother Goddess.
• Its priests and priestesses interpreted the sounds in a sacred oak grove (from birdsong to leaf-rustling) to determine correct actions.
• Later became a shrine to Zeus.

Pachacamac
• A temple site in what is now Peru, 25 miles SE of Lima.
• Pilgrims came to consult the god believed to reside in the temple.
• A resident body of priests handed down the god's pronouncements.
• The shrine was sacked by the Spaniards in the 1530s, but priests had already hidden the treasures.

• • • ANIMALS IN TAI CHI • • •

Many *tai chi* movements are based on animal behaviour. These examples are from the short Yang form – a popular variant of the discipline. Can you spot them next time you see people doing tai chi in the park?

NAME OF THE MOVEMENT	WHAT THE ANIMAL REPRESENTS	BENEFITS OF THE MOVEMENT
Crane spreads its wings	Strength, grace	Stimulates central nervous system and digestion
Carry tiger to mountain	Power, wisdom, tenacity	Develops self-confidence and co-ordination
Repulse monkey	Flexibility, cunning, innovation	Tones upper arms, calves and shoulders; stimulates lymph; increases emotional strength
Snake creeps down	Knowledge, patience, accuracy	Tones thighs and buttocks; lessens frustration and anger
Golden pheasant stands on one leg	Beauty, wisdom	Develops balance; strengthens bones; builds self-confidence
Pat the high horse	Fluidity, freedom, perseverance	Develops balance and co-ordination; strengthens resolve

••• ✿ •••

• • MAKE YOUR OWN CROP CIRCLE • •

You will need:
• A wooden plank with a rope attached to a hole at each end to make a loop long enough to hold in the middle at waist height
• *Or:* A garden roller
• Extra rope as a circle-making guide
• A ball of string
• A tape measure
• A cap with a small wire loop hanging down from the brim
• An accomplice
• A step-ladder

1. Make a sketch of your design, and choose an area with tall grass or crops – ensure you have secured any necessary permissions.

2. With the tape measure, plot your design on the area using string on the ground as a marker.

3. Depress the grass/crops according to your chosen design by pushing or pulling the roller along the ground, or by dragging the loop of rope. To keep straight lines straight, wear the cap, and line up the wire loop with a fixed point directly ahead of you as you walk.

4. For a circle, take a length of rope to match the radius. Hold one end while your accomplice holds the other. Walk 360° around him/her, keeping it taut, and flattening stalks with the plank or roller as you go. Trample more complex parts with your feet.

5. Observe your design from a step-ladder – aerial views are what crop circles are made for!

• • • A CLASSIC TAROT LAYOUT • • •

A number of Tarot card layouts are regularly followed by those using the Tarot for guidance on searching questions, such as "Should I move to the countryside?" or "How can I achieve a promotion at work?" They include the Seven-card Horseshoe and the Tree of Life. Given below are instructions for the classic Celtic Cross. Some Tarot readers like the querent (the seeker) to write out their question and lay it underneath the significator (the card chosen to represent the querent).

1. Choose a "significator" – usually the court card (King, Queen, Knight or Page) that you feel most suits your disposition. Lay this in front of you, face-up.

2. Shuffle the rest of the cards.

3. Lay the deck on the table face-down and use your left hand to cut it into three piles. Still using your left hand, bring the deck back together in a different order.

4. Take the first card off the top (A) and place it face-up on top of the significator to cover it completely. Place the second card (B) face-up across the first (A) – to form a cross.

5. Lay the remaining cards as shown in the diagram opposite, one by one in the order of the letters allotted to them here.

6. Once the cards are in place, proceed with the tricky bit: your personal interpretation of the layout. The individual cards within the layout are generally taken to represent the possibilities shown in the key given here above the layout diagram. Many Tarot readers restrict themselves to the Major Arcana *(see p131 for a table of possible meanings)*, ignoring the Minor Arcana except for the court card used as a significator.

Key to the Tree of Life layout:

A: the central issue affecting the querent

B: the immediate challenge; or an obstacle in the way

C: the roots of the issue in the distant past

D: influences on the issue in the more recent past; experiences that may help with the answer

E: the best that can be achieved

F: what is *likely* to happen in the future; pending events

G: the current situation, and how it feels to the querent

H: external influences; people or circumstances that will affect the outcome; how others see the issue

I: hopes or fears surrounding the issue (often intermingled)

J: the final outcome; how the issue may be resolved; how you will feel in the end

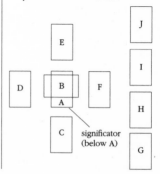

significator (below A)

Mecca, *Saudi Arabia*

Muslims are required to make a *hajj*, or pilgrimage, to the holy city of Mecca, birthplace of the Prophet Mohammed, at least once in their lifetime, circumstances allowing. Every year, over 2 million Muslims travel here to circle the Kaaba and kiss the Black Stone (*see p93*).

Church of the Holy Sepulchre, *Jerusalem, Israel*

A pilgrimage site since the 4th century, this Christian church (with adjoining chapels) is thought to cover the site of Golgotha, where Jesus was crucified, and to incorporate his tomb (sepulchre).

Western Wall, *Jerusalem, Israel*

Also known as the Wailing Wall, this Jewish holy site is the sole survivor of Jerusalem's Second Temple, after its destruction by the Romans. Millions flock here to pray and to squeeze written prayers into its crevices.

Bodh Gaya, *India*

Siddhartha Gautama (who became the Buddha) sat under a tree here and found enlightenment. The ancient Mahabodhi Temple and the bodhi tree (supposedly a direct descendant of the one that sheltered the Buddha) attract thousands of visitors daily.

Santiago de Compostela Cathedral, *NW Spain*

This early medieval cathedral supposedly houses the bones of the Apostle St James. The Way of St James, which leads here, was a major Christian pilgrimage route of the Middle Ages.

Glastonbury, *England*

Believed by Wiccans and other neo-pagans to be the centre of the ancient land of Avalon. There is a theory that the landscape around Glastonbury has the signs of the zodiac mapped out in its features. Major sites include the Tor, the Chalice Well, whose waters are said to be healing, and the Glastonbury Thorn, reputedly grown from Joseph of Arimathea's staff.

Baha'i House of Worship, *Delhi, India*

Sacred to the Baha'i faith, this lotus flower-shaped temple is composed of 27 free-standing white marble-clad "petals", arranged in clusters of three to form nine sides. Completed in 1986, it is already one of the world's most visited buildings (4 million visitors per year). Its four daily prayer sessions feature prayers from various world religions.

Jagannath Temple, *Puri, India*

Millions of Hindus flock to this 12th-century temple every summer for the Ratha Yatra festival, during which three massive wooden statues are placed on giant chariots and paraded. The images represent Jagannatha, an incarnation of the Lord Krishna; his brother Balarama; and their sister Subhadra.

Sri Harmandir Sahib, *Amritsar, India*

Built in the 16th century, this is Sikhism's most sacred site: a sumptuous temple, adorned with gold (alternative name: the Golden Temple). Although in the middle of a small lake, it was built with four doors to show that people of every religion are welcome. Devoted Sikhs pray daily to be able to visit this holy site at least once in their lifetime.

Mount Athos, *N Greece*
An Eastern Orthodox monastic community, with over 2,000 inhabitants in twenty monasteries, dramatically built on a mountain on plugs of rock and accessible only by sea. Monks have lived here since the 4th century. The site was reputedly blessed by the Virgin, who landed nearby after her ship was blown off course. Visiting numbers are strictly controlled. Only men are admitted: women are prohibited, as are female domestic animals.

••• ✳ •••

• • • *STAR SYMBOLS* • • •

Stars tend in general to denote inspiration, hope, achievement or supremacy. However, in particular cultures different forms of star, with various numbers of points from four to seven, have acquired more specific symbolic associations.

Pentagram: Harmony, health and mystic powers. An ancient symbol of life and the Earth Mother. Sacred to the Celtic death goddess the Morrigan. A sign of the earth element (pentacles in the Tarot). A Kabbalistic and neo-pagan talisman of protection. When inverted (with two points at the top), the symbol can represent the Devil's horns, in Satanism.

Hexagram: Union in duality. The union of Kali and Shiva in Hinduism. In the West, the union of God and his spouse (the *shekina* in mystical Judaism). Now widely used as the symbol of Judaism: the star of David (who unified Judah and Israel), formerly known as Solomon's Seal.

Septagram: Cosmic and spiritual order. Derives its symbolism from the sacred and mystical significance of seven. Important in Western Kabbalah, where it symbolizes the sphere of Netzach, the seven planets, the seven alchemical metals, the seven days of the week. In Wicca, the Fairy Star.

Octagram: Regeneration. Linked with Venus, Roman goddess of love and fertility. In the Gnostic tradition, a symbol of creation. In Nordic countries, the eight-pointed star was carved onto doors and walls as a talisman of protection.

Star of the Muses: A nine-pointed star made up of three interlaced triangles. Represents sacred groups of nine women in some traditions – the muses of Greece, the moon maidens of Scandinavian myth, the Korrigans of Celtic myth. A simpler version symbolizes the Baha'i faith (*see pp116–17*).

• SOLUTION-FOCUSED THERAPY •

Traditional psychotherapy can take years to produce results. However, some new forms turn their backs on delving into the past and claim that six months will be enough to deal with most issues. Solution-focused therapy (or "brief therapy") aims to bring out our inherent problem-solving faculty. One technique focuses on the "miracle question":

1. If you woke one morning and all your problems had vanished, how would you know this "miracle" had happened? What would it feel like? Consider how the new situation would affect your state of mind.

2. Ask yourself, in what ways would you behave differently from before?

3. Once this miracle had happened, how would your family and friends behave differently?

4. What differences do you think your family and friends would see in you and your behaviour?

5. Are there any parts of this miracle that are already happening in your life, even if only occasionally?

6. If so, how have you made these things happen, and what actions could you take to achieve this kind of result more often, or permanently?

7. What parts of your life at the moment would you like to continue as they are?

8. On a scale of 0 to 10 (where 0 is the worst your life has ever been and 10 is the day after the miracle), where are you now?

9. How might you progress by just one point up this scale? What would you need to do differently?

10. How would your family and friends know when you had moved up the scale by one point?

••• ✵ •••

• THE TEN AVATARS OF VISHNU •

In Hindu thought, higher beings, or *devi*, manifest themselves on Earth through successive incarnations known as *avatars*. Below are the ten generally accepted *avatars* of Vishnu, the "preserver" god:

Matsya, *the fish*
Kurma, *the tortoise*
Varaha, *the boar*
Narasimha, *the half-man, half-lion*
Vamana, *the dwarf*
Parashurama, *meaning "Rama with the axe"*
Rama, *the prince and king of Ayodhya*
Krishna, *the "all-attractive one"*
Buddha, *the "enlightened one"*
Kalki, *the "destroyer of foulness"*

• • • *NOTABLE CARGO CULTS* • • •

Cargo cults are localized faiths that have emerged in some tribal societies, mostly in the islands of the SW Pacific, following initial encounters with outsiders from more "advanced" countries. Impressed by manufactured goods, or "cargo", that they observed during such encounters, some native peoples presumed that these items had been created by supernatural means. They sought to obtain similar wealth by performing sacred magic, including ceremonies that mimicked Western ways. Some cults still exist today.

Vailala Madness
(Territory of Papua, Papuan Gulf, 1919–after 1922)
The name of this cult came from observations of its participants, who spoke in tongues (fluent, speech-like but unintelligible utterances) and displayed shaking tendencies. Members believed that a "Ghost Steamer" piloted by the returning ancestors (who would be white) would bring tinned food, tools and other resources. Western traditions and the idea of "cargo" are thought to have been picked up by leaders of the movement while working abroad in plantations.

Tuka Movement
(Fiji, 1885–early 1900s)
This began when a Fijian priest, called Ndugomoi, reacted against the influence of Christian missionaries. He renamed himself Navosavakandua ("he who speaks once"), proclaimed himself supreme judge of all things and predicted that native ancestors would return to expel the white settlers, restoring the natural order of things.

John Frum Cult
(Island of Tanna, Vanuatu, 1930s–present day)
Members believe that John Frum, an American World War II serviceman, will bring wealth and prosperity to the people if they follow him. However, it's unclear whether this man actually ever existed. The name could be a corruption of "John from (America)". A native named Manehivi started the cult, calling himself John Frum, and encouraging locals to reject Christianity and celebrate traditional customs. After American troops were stationed in Vanuatu in the 1940s, other figures such as Uncle Sam, Santa Claus and John the Baptist were also seen as figures who would bring cargo wealth to the island.

Prince Philip Movement
(Island of Tanna, Vanuatu, 1950s/60s–present day)
Members of the Yaohnanen tribe believe Prince Philip to be the pale-skinned son of a mountain spirit and the brother of John Frum. According to ancient tales, the mountain spirit's son travelled to a distant land, married a powerful lady and will, in time, return. The villagers observed the respect accorded to Queen Elizabeth II by colonial officials and concluded that her husband, Prince Philip, must be the son who featured in their legends. These beliefs were reinforced by a royal visit to the island in 1974.

... LIVING IN TUNE WITH ...
THE LUNAR CYCLE

In antiquity the moon was thought to influence plant growth. Even today many gardeners follow moon-planting manuals telling when to plant and harvest each crop. Rudolf Steiner's biodynamic farming methods follow similar principles. In the same spirit, many today use the guidance of the moon for healthy living, according to the following precepts:

Waning moon: Ideal for detoxification, losing weight, having your hair cut or your legs waxed (the skin won't get red and sore). The best time for operations, as healing is swifter and scars less severe. Also good for visiting the dentist – plaque is more easily removed, crowns and bridges last longer, and extractions are less painful.

Waxing moon: At this time the body absorbs everything put into it, so heavy, sweet or fatty foods are best avoided. Vitamin and mineral supplements will be absorbed more effectively than at other times. Insect bites and stings are more painful; poisons have a stronger effect.

New moon: Perfect for giving up bad habits, as withdrawal symptoms will be less severe than at other times. Also suitable for new ventures, whether in relationships, careers or business.

Full moon: Ideal for nourishing the body with moisturizing treatments, oil massages and herbal soaks. Vaccinations or operations should be avoided; also confrontations are likely, as emotions run high and tempers can flare.

• • • THE EIGHT LIMBS OF YOGA • • •

The physical yoga postures (*asana*) – which many in the West often think of as "yoga" in its entirety – are, in fact, only one of the "eight limbs" of yoga practice, as outlined in Patanjali's *Yoga Sutras* (*see p76*). These eight yogic "limbs" function as practical guidelines on how to live a more meaningful, fulfilling and contented life:

Yama: Positive conduct toward others and the outside world
Niyama: Positive conduct and attitude toward ourselves
Asana: Physical postures
Pranayama: Breathing practices
Pratyahara: Withdrawal of the senses to develop internal awareness
Dharana: Concentration, when the mind is oriented toward
a single object
Dhyana: Meditation, the unbroken flow of consciousness toward
a single object
Samadhi: Bliss, or deep meditation, when only the object of
meditation is apparent

HOW TO PERFORM
INDIAN HEAD MASSAGE

Indian Head Massage is an appealing home treatment to give or receive: not only is it safe and easy to learn, but it has a range of benefits, from stress relief and headache prevention to general enhancement of emotional well-being. The subject should sit on a chair, while the masseur stands behind him or her. For best results, use warm sesame or coconut oil.

Caution: This treatment should not be performed on areas of the body where there are open cuts or sores, or weeping eczema/psoriasis.

1. Apply the massage oil to your hands and slowly rub your subject's scalp with the pads of your fingertips.

2. Support the back of his or her head with one hand and move the palm of your other hand in a swift but gentle rubbing motion, as if buffing a window: start at the base of one ear and work upward, across the midline of the head and down to the other ear. Repeat in the other direction.

3. Use sweeping movements to "comb" the hair, running your fingernails through it in long strokes. Work all the way around the head, swapping hands if necessary.

4. Gently move your thumbs in small circling movements to simultaneously massage both sides of the neck: start

where the neck joins the skull and work downward.

5. Massage the temples with the tips of your index fingers, again in small circular movements. Then support the back of your subject's head with your hands and massage the temples again – this time with a slightly firmer pressure.

6. Imagine you are ironing your subject's shoulders, using the heel of each hand to roll from the back to the front of the shoulder. Do this first at the outside edge, gradually moving in toward the collarbone. Do either one shoulder at a time or both together.

7. Put both hands around the head like a cap. Squeeze, lift and let go several times. (This technique alone can be used to combat headaches.)

8. Stroke your palms lightly down your subject's whole face – from forehead to chin – to encourage deeper relaxation.

9. Cover his or her eyes with your palms, pressing gently with the heels of your hands on the closed eyelids. If you're giving the massage before bedtime, finish at this point to help to send the subject off to sleep. (This technique alone can be used to combat insomnia.)

10. If, on the other hand, your subject wishes to be left feeling energized, use a brisk rubbing motion back and forth across the whole scalp. Vary this with a fast but gentle scratching action, using your fingernails. Both can be quite firm and deep.

11. Finish by pressing firmly but carefully on the crown.

• HOW TO MASTER LUCID DREAMING •

Lucid dreaming occurs when you become *aware* that you're dreaming. With practice, the dreamer can take control of elements of the dream – for example, deciding to pick up a pen and write with it. Some people find this easier than others. However, with practice and persistence, anyone can master the technique and learn how to control their dream world. Here are some effective ways to encourage this:

Dream journal: It's easier to become lucid in a familiar dream landscape, so keep a dream journal to help you remember, noting all your dreams as soon as you wake up – their symbols, their settings, their moods and details. Keep the journal by your bedside. Try drawing any recurrent landscapes to fix them in your mind.

again clearly. Tell yourself that when you next see them, you'll be dreaming – and you'll be aware that you are. This technique commonly takes upward of three months of practice, but it does work in the end.

Anchoring: Give your mind a conscious prompt to help it to recognize when it's in dream mode. One way to do this is to look at your hands frequently during the day. Close your eyes whenever you have a spare minute and practise *visualizing* your hands. As you're getting ready to sleep, visualize them

Autosuggestion: When you awake from a dream in the night, go over it several times until it's as clear as possible in your mind. Just before you drift off to sleep again, tell yourself: "Next time I'm dreaming, I want to recognize that I'm dreaming." Visualize yourself back in the dream you had earlier but clearly realizing you're dreaming it. Repeat this declaration to yourself several times until your intention is firmly fixed in your mind.

••• ❀ •••

• • • WHO WAS CONFUCIUS? • • •

• A philosopher born in 551BCE in the small feudal state of Lu, in what is now Shantung province, China.

• He stressed the need for a harmonious society and a benevolent state within a well-defined hierarchy.

• Among his key teachings were: *li* (propriety and ritual), *xiao* (filial piety, also used as a template for other relationships), *zhong* (loyalty to oneself, others and the state) and, above all other principles, *ren* (humaneness, goodness).

• His teachings were compiled in texts, notably *Analects of Confucius*, by loyal disciples, such as Mencius and Xunzi.

• He died in 479BCE before his ideas gained prominence during the Han Dynasty (206BCE–220CE).

... THE MYTHICAL ORIGINS ...
OF THE TIBETAN PEOPLE

A saintly monkey once journeyed to the Himalayas to enjoy undisturbed meditation in a remote cave called Zodang Gongpori, above the town of Tsetang. A rock-demoness who lived nearby became entranced by his piety and serenity and fell in love with him. However, the monkey, who had sworn a vow of chastity, politely ignored her flattery and her attempts to seduce him.

The demoness was tormented by this unrequited love, and after some time the monkey began to feel sympathy for her. He was also justifiably worried about the danger an angry demoness could cause to the world. So he became her consort. Their union produced six children, who represented the six levels of sentient being. These offspring multiplied to become four hundred, dividing into six tribes. The six tribes then divided themselves into twelve kingdoms and 40 principalities. It's said that the entire population of Tibet is descended from these tribes.

• FOUR TYPES OF DETOX •

Naturopaths use various forms of fasting and detoxification to help bring the body back to a state of balance. The following are some of the most commonly prescribed treatments. However, you should check with your doctor before undergoing any kind of detox, and it's important to have professional supervision throughout.

Water fasting
Consuming only water, no food. It can be used to treat certain health conditions and also for weight loss. However, after 24 hours your body starts to take its energy not only from stored fat but also from muscle, so you need to exercise caution.

Juice fasting
Consuming only freshly squeezed fruit and vegetable juice (and water). Fruits and vegetables are rich in micro-nutrients; many actively encourage elimination of toxins. Taking them in liquid rather than solid form makes for easier digestion. Often recommended for rheumatism or arthritis. Usually done for up to a week.

Mono-diets
Spending a day or more on just one type of raw fruit or vegetable (depending on your particular health problem, as advised by an expert).

You eat the whole fruit or vegetable, and drink its juice – consuming as much as you like. This also aids weight loss.

Exclusion diets
Following a highly restricted diet (under expert guidance) for about a month, then slowly, systematically reintroducing other foods and recording the effects they have on your mind and body. Designed to pinpoint any food intolerances.

• • • *THE FENG SHUI PA KUA* • • •

The energy, (*qi* or *chi*), of a space is associated with the main points of the compass, known in feng shui as the Eight Locations. The *pa kua*, meaning "eight shapes", is a template showing the qualities, elements and colours associated with each Location. In the centre is an area known as the *tai chi*, or "earthpot", which has yin and yang energies swirling around it (see below).

By laying the pa kua over a floorplan of your home, you identify which rooms fall into which pa kua sectors. This enables you to assess and work on the chi in that room and in the process create a more appropriate environment for daily living.

Problems in a certain area of your life might be accounted for by energy blockage or leakage. If, for example, your bathroom falls in the "wealth" area (southeast), this may explain financial problems: your money going "down the drain". It's probably not feasible to relocate your bathroom, but small measures can help, such as keeping the toilet lid closed when not in use (to avoid energy leakage) and placing a mirror on the outside of the bathroom door (to reflect chi back into the house, rather than letting it escape via the bathroom). In a similar vein, growing a plant in whatever room falls in your "creativity" area (west) can encourage inspiration. Or hanging a picture of a mountain in your "career" area (north) might inspire you to conquer a challenge.

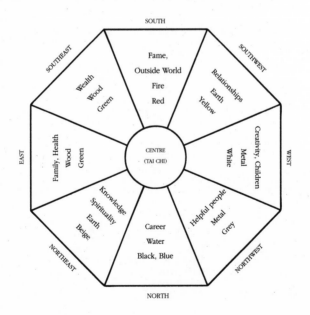

• *THE TWELVE LABOURS OF HERAKLES* •

The twelve labours of the Greek hero Herakles (Hercules to the Romans) were imposed by his cousin Eurystheus, king of Tiryns, to make him atone for the murder of his own family in a fit of madness. Initially only ten labours were set, but Eurystheus subsequently added two more, claiming that Herakles had taken payment for cleaning the Augean stables and had received help in killing the Lernean Hydra.

Killing the Nemean lion,
the hide of which was invulnerable; he throttled the beast.

Slaying the Lernean Hydra,
which grew two heads for every one removed; he seared the flesh with a torch to prevent more heads from growing.

Capturing the Kerynian hind,
a golden-horned deer sacred to the goddess Artemis; he chased it for a whole year before catching it.

Capturing the giant Erymanthian boar,
by driving it into thick snow.

Cleaning the Augean stables,
by diverting two rivers to wash away the dung.

Driving off the man-eating Stymphalian birds
infesting Lake Stymphalos in Arcadia; he used a bronze rattle to make them fly, then shot them with a bow and arrow.

Capturing the Cretan bull,
which was ravaging the island of Crete; he overcame it with ease.

Stealing King Diomedes' four man-eating mares,
by killing the king and feeding him to the beasts.

Fetching the girdle of Hippolyta, Queen of the Amazons,
by impressing her so much that she handed it over voluntarily.

Capturing the cattle of the giant Geryon,
by killing first his two-headed guard-dog Orthrus, then Geryon himself.

Fetching the golden apples of the Hesperides,
by persuading the giant Atlas to pick them, while he held up the heavens in Atlas's place.

Capturing the three-headed guard-dog Cerberus from the Underworld,
by using brute strength, after which he showed the beast to Eurystheus and returned it to avoid offence to Hades.

• THE WHEEL OF THE YEAR •

Wiccans and other pagans celebrate eight major festivals throughout the year, including those observed by the Celts in antiquity:

Samhain/Hallowe'en:
October 31
The Celtic New Year: the death of the old year and (re)birth of the new. A celebration of the Goddess in her Crone aspect (*see p73*). A time of purification and renewal. The veils between our world and that of the dead are said to be thin at this time. Divination and quiet introspective work are often undertaken.

Yule/Winter Solstice:
December 21
The shortest day and longest night of the year. The festival of the rebirth of the sun. The Oak King, Lord of Summer, is reborn, taking over from the Holly King, Lord of Winter, after defeating him in battle. A family festival all about the hearth, home and loved ones.

Imbolc/Candlemas:
February 2
The Goddess returns in her Maiden aspect (*see p73*) as the early signs of spring are seen. Nature seems dead; yet beneath the earth, life is stirring.

A festival about trust, hope, dreams and journeying within oneself to find inner resources.

Oestre/Spring Equinox: *March 21*
A time of balance when day and night are equal. The festival of the Saxon goddess Oestre, the Goddess of the Egg. A festival about opening up and seizing new opportunities in life. A time for spring-cleaning, both physically and mentally – eliminating the old to make room for the new.

Beltane/May Day:
May 1
The festival of the fire god Bel. Traditionally, old hearth fires were extinguished and new ones kindled from the central Bel fire. The marriage of the God and Goddess takes place, and the Goddess takes on her Mother aspect (*see p73*). A major fertility festival that celebrates sensuality, energy and freedom. This is also the festival of vows or contracts, and is a traditional time for pagan marriages.

Litha/Summer Solstice: *June 21*
The longest day and shortest night of the year. The battle of the Oak and Holly Kings is enacted, but this time the Holly King wins. A festival about people coming together and helping to heal society. Many pagans sit in vigil for the sun all night.

Lughnasadh/Lammas: *August 1*
The festival of the dying and rising God. Lammas is a Saxon name, from Loafmas – the first loaf of the harvest (when the first corn is cut). At this festival, thanks are offered to the Corn King for giving his life to feed humankind.

Mabon/Autumn Equinox:
September 21
Another time of balance, with equal day and night. A festival of harvest and purification, before winter, when the Goddess, in her Crone aspect, begins her descent to the Underworld (later to return as the Maiden). A time for forgiveness, and moving on.

✦✦✦✦✦✦✦

• • • *BLOOD-TYPE DIETS* • • •

Some nutritional therapists and naturopaths, such as Dr Peter Adamo, author of *Eat Right 4 Your Type*, advocate adjusting your diet according to your blood type. This table shows the various blood types and what people with each blood type should and shouldn't eat.

TYPE	WHO WERE THEY?	WHAT ARE THEIR HEALTH ISSUES?	WHAT SHOULD THEY EAT?	WHAT SHOULD THEY RESTRICT?
O	Hunter-gatherers, dating back 200,000 years	Low thyroid, ulcers, allergies, arthritis, fatigue	Fish, meat, vegetables, fruit	Dairy produce, wheat, corn, oranges
A	The first farmers, dating back 10,000 years	Cancer, diabetes, heart disease, anaemia	Grains, legumes, pulses (not kidney beans), fruit, seafood	Dairy produce, wheat, meat, kidney beans
B	Originated when Caucasian and Mongolian tribes mixed, 10–15,000 years ago	Multiple sclerosis, lupus, diabetes, immune disorders	Dairy, legumes, pulses (not lentils), meat, vegetables, fruit	Poultry, peanuts, lentils, buckwheat, corn, wheat
AB	Blend of type A and B: only 1,000 years old	Cancer, anaemia, heart disease	Dairy, pulses (not kidney beans), meat, seafood, vegetables, fruit	Corn, seeds, red meat, kidney beans

••• ❁ •••

• • • *LABYRINTHS AND MAZES* • • •

The earliest labyrinths were unicursal (1), which means that one single route leads to the centre and out again – with no possibility of getting lost. This type was (and still is) used for contemplation and meditation. Later, multicursal mazes (2) developed, in which many paths are dead-ends, with the result that choices continually have to be made about which direction to take. These were designed to puzzle and confuse. They were often used in initiation ceremonies: going into the maze symbolized death, or the end of an era; and coming out, rebirth.

1.

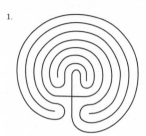

2.

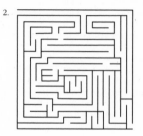

• • • SOME FAMOUS MEDIUMS • • •

Helena Blavatsky (1831–1891)

Even as a child, Ukrainian-born Madame Blavatksy saw phantoms and imaginary hunchbacked friends. As an adult, she spent ten years travelling the world, before moving to New York, where she proved her psychic abilities, including mediumship, levitation, clairvoyance, telepathy and materialization (creating physical objects out of nothing). She co-founded the Theosophical Society, for the promotion of spiritual wisdom and universal brotherhood, in 1875.

Edgar Cayce (1877–1945)

From his childhood in Kentucky, USA, Cayce's psychic abilities were evident: he was able to see and talk to his late grandfather's spirit. As an adult, he became known as the "sleeping prophet": while lying in a self-induced sleep-like state, he claimed to be able to contact anyone in the world, from any time in history, answer any question, make prophecies and diagnose illnesses.

The Fox Sisters

- **Kate** (1838–1892)
- **Leah** (1814–1890)
- **Margaret** (1836–1893)

The Fox sisters claimed that they could communicate with a spirit who lived in their house in Hydesville, New York, USA, using mysterious knocks and raps. Bones were found in their cellar, thought to be the remains of a murdered peddler. They conducted public séances that were attended by many celebrities of the day, including Sir Arthur Conan Doyle and James Fenimore Cooper.

Eusapia Palladino (1854–1918)

Palladino was originally from Naples, Italy, where she was at one stage married to an itinerant magician. She travelled all over Europe, conducting séances in darkened rooms, and displaying other psychic powers, including levitation and playing musical instruments without touching them. She claimed to be under the control of a spirit named John King. She was investigated by numerous scientists (including Pierre and Marie Curie), who drew varying conclusions as to her authenticity.

Chico Xavier (1910–2002)

One of the most prominent members of the Brazilian Spiritism movement, Xavier was led by a spirit guide named Emmanuel. He was famous for his use of "psychography" – allowing his writing hand to be guided by spirits. Using this technique, alternatively known as "automatic writing", he authored more than 400 books.

Stanisława Tomczyk (c.1890–mid-20th century)

This Polish medium claimed to be controlled by a mischievous being called "Little Stasia". She was telekinetic (able to move objects without touching them). She could stop the movement of cased clocks and influence the turn of a roulette wheel. The scientist Julian Ochorowicz subjected her to rigorous experiments in 1908–09, at Wisła, Poland, and concluded that her abilities were the result of solid "rays" projecting from her fingers.

Clifford Bias (1910–87)
Born in West Virginia, USA,
Bias was able to speak to
the dead from the age of 5.
Popular across the United
States, he reportedly advised the
Roosevelts. He established the
Universal Spiritualist Association,
the Spiritualist-Episcopal Church,
and also the Ancient Mystical
Order of Seekers – a society for
magic and the occult.

Allison DuBois (b.1972)
From Arizona, USA, DuBois
is among the most popular
of the world's living mediums.
She first communicated with
deceased souls at the age of 6,
and now aims to put the living
in touch with loved ones who
have passed away. She has also
worked with the police to help
to solve crimes. The TV show
Medium is based on her life.

••• ❁ •••

• STANDING ON YOUR SHOULDERS •

Shoulderstand (*Sarvangasana*) is one of the inverted yoga *asanas* that stretch the upper back and neck, tone the legs and buttocks, give the heart a chance to rest, improve digestion and boost blood supply to the brain. It can also enhance energy, relieve stress, increase concentration and relaxation, and alleviate insomnia. However, it's an intermediate pose, so must be learned with an experienced instructor. Here are some practice reminders, once you are able to do it alone:

1. Lie on the floor, or on a folded blanket with your shoulders on the blanket and your head on the floor. Bend your knees with your feet flat on the floor, then lift your knees in toward your chest, with your palms on the floor by your sides.

2. Press your arms into the floor, engage your stomach muscles and gently rock your hips off the floor toward your face, spreading your palms on your lower back for support and bringing your elbows as close as you can on the floor. Hang your heels by your buttocks and

aim to bring your back to a vertical position.

3. Once you're steady and comfortable in step 2, slowly lift your legs straight up, to bring them into a vertical line with your body. Tuck in your pelvis to help with this. Keep your feet together and walk your hands up your back (toward the floor). Softly gaze at your chest but do not move your head.

4. Stay here for up to 30 seconds initially. Aim to add on about 5 seconds every day you practise until you can hold the pose for 3 minutes.

Caution: Don't practise this pose if you have high blood pressure, neck problems, diarrhoea or a headache, or if you're menstruating. Avoid Shoulderstand if you're pregnant.

Latin, or Protestant, Cross

Originally a pagan symbol. The vertical axis indicates spirit; the horizontal, the material world. Now the emblem of Christ's Passion.

Ankh, or Egyptian, Cross

Emerged in ancient Egypt as the hieroglyph for "life", also representing sexual union and the immortality of the gods. Since adopted by many groups, including Rosicrucians and Coptic Christians.

Celtic Cross

According to legend, introduced to Ireland by St Patrick. In fact, its origins may be pre-Christian, dating back to the sun crosses of the Bronze Age. In Hinduism, known as the *kiakra*: a sign of sexual union – the phallic cross within the yoni circle.

Sun, Odin's or Wheel Cross

Found scratched on cave walls dating back as far as the Stone Age. Bronze Age cultures also used it, perhaps identifying it with the four-spoked wheels of chariots in use by that time. Later adopted by the Cathars of medieval Europe. Also found in Native North American cultures, representing the wheel of life.

Fleur de Lis Cross

Incorporates stylized designs of an iris or lily. This cross has long been associated with the French monarchy; nowadays it is linked with their Spanish Bourbon relatives. Shown with extended arms it becomes the Fleury or Flourished Cross, familiar in heraldry.

Papal, or Maronite, Cross

Also known as the ferula, an emblem of the papal office. The three horizontal bars represent the pope's triple role as bishop of Rome, patriarch of the Catholic Church and successor of St Peter, although the third was more likely to have been added to distinguish the papal staff from the two-barred crosses

associated with archbishops.

Canterbury Cross

So called from the shape featured on an Anglo-Saxon brooch dating from c.850 dug up in Canterbury, England, in 1867. Four arms of identical shape and size widen as they extend outward, with a circular form to the extremities. A stone replica now stands in Canterbury Cathedral.

St Brigid's Cross

Popular in Ireland, where it represents the cross of reeds woven by Brigid, the daughter of a pagan chieftain, in her attempts to convert people to Christianity in the 6th century. Others link the symbol with Brigid, the Celtic goddess of fire and poetry. St Brigid's Crosses are still sometimes used as talismans to protect houses from fire.

St John's, or Maltese, Cross

Formed of four identically shaped arrowheads joining at their tips, this became the symbol of the Knights of St John, a crusading order also known as the Knights Hospitaller. When the last crusaders were driven from the Holy Land in 1291, the Hospitallers moved to Rhodes and then, in 1530, to Malta – hence the name by which the cross is now known. It's thought to have been linked originally to the ancient Greek concept of *omphalos*, the centre of the world, and associated with goddess worship.

. . . *THE PRINCIPAL HINDU* . . .
SPIRITUAL TEXTS

The Vedas
The oldest texts – in effect, the Hindu scriptures. Thought to have been divinely revealed – *sruti* ("heard"), not *smriti* ("remembered"). Each of the four Vedas is supplemented by *brahmanas* (exegeses), in turn supplemented by *aranyakas* – commentaries on rituals considered so dangerous that they could be studied only in the wilderness.

The Rig Veda: A collection of sacred songs and hymns of praise to the gods – used by the priests known as *hotr*, reciters of invocations and litanies.

The Yajurveda: Ritual formulae used by the *adhvaryu* priests, who performed animal sacrifices.

The Samaveda: Songs of the *udgatr*, or chanting priests, whose central role was to offer libations of the sacred liquid known as *soma* to the deities.

The Atharvaveda: Less directly connected with ritual than the other three Vedas. A collection of hymns, songs of praise, stories and healing formulae whose study was considered dangerous by some believers.

The smriti
Second in authority only to the Vedas, these "remembered" texts are much more numerous. They include:

The Puranas: These secondary texts feature historical, geographical, cosmological and mythical material. Each of the eighteen puranas is dedicated to one of the three major Hindu gods: Vishnu, Shiva or Brahma.

The Epics: India's two great early epics, the *Mahabharata* and the *Ramayana*, include much religious material. The *Mahabharata* incorporates the *Bhagavad Gita* ("Song of the Lord"), a supreme expression of Hinduism.

The Agamas: Doctrinal texts that spell out the spiritual knowledge underlying the worship of the principal Hindu gods. The main sources of yogic instruction. Each one has four parts: philosophical basis of the cult; yogic practices; building and decoration of temples; rites, rituals, festivals.

The Darshanas: Philosophical writings that seek to develop and systematize the message of the Vedas.

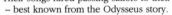

• WATER SPIRITS OF THE WORLD •

Sirens
In ancient Greek myth, birds with the heads, upper
bodies and sometimes arms of beautiful women.
Their songs lured passing sailors to their deaths
– best known from the Odysseus story.

Selkies
Seals that could shed their skins to take human form.
Believed to inhabit the waters off the Orkney Islands,
N and W Scotland, Ireland and Iceland. They needed
their sealskins to change back to animal form: thus,
anyone who purloined the skin had them in their
power. Selkies often take human partners in the tales.

Bunyips
Haunting the rivers, creeks, billabongs and swamps
of Australia, these were hairy-bodied, with dog-like
faces, seal-flippers and walrus-like tusks. They had
voracious appetites and the strength to pull people
and animals down to great depths.

Kappas
Creatures of Japanese legend, with the bodies and shells
of tortoises, arms and legs of frogs, and monkey-like
faces. Amphibious; of superhuman strength. They had a
taste for children's entrails: parents would tell of kappas
to prevent children from playing near water.

Kelpies
Water-horses from Scottish mythology (parallels in
Wales, Ireland, Scandinavia). Saddled and bridled,
they waited at the roadside for travellers to mount
them. They would then take off and plunge into a
loch. Neither horse nor rider would be seen again.

Nagas
Cobra-like, sometimes seven-headed demi-gods of Indian
tradition, who lived in underwater palaces studded with
jewels. Female nagas were celebrated for their beauty
when in mortal guise and took earthly husbands. They
could choose either to help or to harm their human
contacts, depending on the treatment they received.

Nixies
Beautiful freshwater mermaids who lured men to death
by drowning. To attract their prey, they kept their tails
concealed beneath the water. Known in Germany as
nixe, in the Slav lands as *rusalki*.

FOUR CHARACTERISTICS OF MYSTICAL EXPERIENCES

The American psychologist and philosopher **William James** (1842–1910), brother of the novelist Henry James, believed that four general characteristics tend to underline all mystical experiences, whatever the culture or religion in which they occur:

Ineffability

Mystical experiences are beyond the scope of reason and therefore impossible to explain accurately in words – they are felt emotionally. Most mystical literature relies on symbolism, poetry and paradox to express the inexpressible.

Noetic (inner knowing) quality

Mystical experiences convey a transcendent truth – often an awareness of unity with the Absolute, the Divine. An insight or revelation has taken place, beyond what our ordinary understanding is capable of. This revelation has a sense of authority about it.

Transience

Mystical experiences are relatively fleeting. James wrote: "Except in rare instances, half an hour, or at most an hour or two, seems to be the limit beyond which they fade into the light of common day."

Passivity

Mystical experiences are transporting, taking the subject beyond the self. You feel that you are in the control of a superior power, your own will in abeyance. Unlike prophetic speech, automatic writing or trance states, the mystic state is always remembered, and believed to have been important. The person's state of mind can be permanently altered.

••• ❁ •••

ROMAN DEITIES: CHILD GUARDIANS

Every Roman was considered to have a Genius (if male) or a Juno (if female). This was the creative force that watched over the person's development, protected them and formed their personality. In childhood it was joined by various other tutelary spirits, as follows:

Nundina	presided over the child's purification
Vaticanus	made the baby utter its first cry
Cuba	quietened the baby in its cradle
Ossipago	oversaw the development of the child's bones
Carna	oversaw the development of the child's flesh
Educa and Potina	taught the child to eat and drink
Abeona and Adeona	taught the child to walk
Sentinus	awoke the child's intellect

• JUNG'S DREAM OF THE HOUSE •

One of the classic ideas of the Swiss psychologist **Carl Gustav Jung** (1875–1961) is the collective unconscious (*see p59*). A dream he had on board ship as he returned to Europe from the USA with Sigmund Freud in 1909 helped him to formulate this concept. He recorded the dream in his autobiography, *Memories, Dreams, Reflections*. Here is a summary:

He finds himself in what is supposed to be "his house", which appears to have only two storeys. The upper storey is a bright, stylish salon but, when he descends to the ground floor, everything is dark and medieval. He then finds a heavy door, behind which lies a stone stairway to the cellar, so he descends further. He realizes that the walls here date from Roman times and finds a ring in the stone floor slabs, which, when he pulls it, lifts to reveal another stone stairway, this time very narrow. He goes down and finds himself in a low cave cut into the rock, with thick dust on the floor, among which lie scattered bones and broken pottery. He also discovers two old, half-disintegrated human skulls. Then he awakens.

Jung saw this dream as a "short summary" of the life of his psyche: a new way of viewing the mind. The salon represented the conscious mind, the ground floor the first level of the unconscious, and his descent into the hidden, lower levels of the house his exploration into the *deeper* levels of the unconscious. The cave he eventually reached denotes the lowest layer of the psyche (deep in our unconscious, and often neglected): the realm of the primitive human within each of us, with its primordial images and urges. This he came to call the collective unconscious.

••• ❀ •••

• THE FIVE PILLARS OF ISLAM •

The Five Pillars of Islam are the essential duties that all devoted Muslims are expected to perform – the foundation of Muslim life:

Shahada: the Profession of Faith (in Allah alone)
Salah: Ritual Prayers
Zakah: Alms-giving
Sawm: Fasting
Hajj: Pilgrimage to Mecca (see p93)

• WHAT WAS THE BUDDHA LIKE? •

The earliest images of the Buddha in the 5th century BCE are from NW India, in present-day Pakistan and Afghanistan, dating from about 500 years after his death. Many are from the Gandhara region, where Greco-Roman influences from the time of Alexander the Great resulted in the Buddha being depicted as a moustached semi-European.

Later, in central India, in the Gupta period (c. early 3rd to 6th century CE), we see the sublime depictions of meditating and teaching Buddhas, the exquisite symmetries of which express the inner confidence and wisdom associated with an enlightened consciousness.

While we cannot recapture a precise idea of the Buddha's appearance, we do gain a vivid mental picture from accounts of his life written in Pali hundreds of years after his death. He is said to have been a fine, golden-skinned prince, who, on renouncing his court life and seeking spiritual fulfilment, shaved his head, took to wearing yellow robes, and spent his days walking the dusty roads of northern India, carrying a begging bowl.

As for his character, according to the Pali *sutras* (scriptures), it was not that of the conventionally gentle saint. Rather, he was contentious, assertive and often insistent on his own rightness. He was also enormously charismatic, radiating the experience of revelation and making it his mission to enable the same experience for others. Although illiterate, he is believed to have had an ability to talk with ease to anyone – princes, merchants, artisans or fellow monastics – most probably in an unwritten language of the time called Maghadi.

••• ❀ •••

• THE THREE JEWELS OF TAOISM •

Taoism, along with Buddhism and Confucianism, was one of the principal spiritual traditions of feudal China. At the core of its teachings is the *Tao Te Ching*, attributed to the sage **Lao Tzu** (c.604–c.531BCE). It is in this respected text that the Three Jewels, or Three Treasures, of Taoism were first identified:

慈	儉	不敢為天下先
Compassion (*ci*) Empathizing with the sufferings of others, showing kindness to them and helping with their problems – based on the understanding that all things are interconnected. Lao Tzu comments that *ci* can lead to courage.	**Moderation** (*jian*) A wholesome, modest way of life; commitment to avoiding excess or overindulgence of any kind. Lao Tzu remarks that this can lead to generosity, because people who are frugal tend to have more to give.	**Humility** (*bugan wei tianxia xian*) Literally described as "daring not to be ahead of others". A belief that the best way to lead, in spiritual terms, is by humbly setting an example. This helps to keep us safe to fulfil our potential.

Water is widely believed to have cleansing, renewing or healing powers. It symbolizes fertility, and the fluidity of earthly forms. Reverence for water is especially marked where the resource is scarce, as shown by Jewish, Islamic, Christian and Indian rites. A spring was considered a point where creation came to the surface and humans could touch the divine.

Lourdes, *Hautes-Pyrénées, France:* In 1858, the 14-year-old peasant girl Bernadette Soubirous saw the Virgin Mary appear 18 times at a grotto here, called Massabieille. Guided by Mary, she began to dig until a small pool of water appeared. Gradually this grew to become the sacred, healing spring for which Lourdes is famous. Five million people a year visit to drink or bathe in the waters, and more than 70 miraculous cures have been recorded by the Medical Bureau here. The crowds soon outgrew the chapel built above the grotto in 1876; an immense new church, holding some 20,000, was built in 1958.

Nachi, *Kii Katsuura, Wakayama Prefecture, Japan:* A waterfall associated with a shrine of the Kumano (Buddhist-Shinto) faith, whose followers aspired to a long life and rebirth in paradise. Originally, the shrine was right at the foot of the waterfall, which was revered as a nature deity, or *kami*.

The Ganges, *India:* Ganga Mai (Mother Ganges) is viewed as the personification of the Hindu goddess Ganga. Its waters are thought to have descended from heaven through a lock of Shiva's hair. Ganges water is supremely sacred, purifying everything and everyone it touches. To bathe in it is to be blessed and absolved of sin. Sited on the river is Varanasi, considered the holiest city in Hinduism, with hundreds of temples along the shores. The most famous Ganges festival is the Kumbh Mela, which takes place four times every twelve years, each time at one of four sacred locations.

Well of Sacrifice, *Chichén Itzá, Yucatán, Mexico:* One of the most famous *cenotes* – natural sink holes viewed as sacred in the Mayan tradition. Believed to be the navel of the world and the entrance to the underworld. Excavations in the early 1900s yielded sacrificial objects (gold, obsidian and jade ornaments, clay vessels) and evidence of human sacrifice – probably to the rain gods (Chaacs).

Bakau, *The Gambia:* The sacred pool, established five centuries ago, is the focus of a fertility rite that draws women from all over Africa, and beyond. It is home to around 80 (fish-eating) crocodiles, deliberately introduced as requested by the spirit of the pool. Visitors are washed with the sacred water by the pool's keepers, women from the Bojang clan; offerings of cloth and coconuts are given in return. As well as curing infertility, the waters are said to bring general good fortune.

• ANCIENT CHINA'S FIVE ELEMENTS •

The Chinese believed that the human body, and the whole world, was composed of five basic elements (*wu xing*), all with mystic significance:

Earth 土
Balance of yin and yang. Associated with thoughtfulness and patience, harmony and stability. In excess, can cause anxiety.

Wood Yang 木
or masculine. Associated with strength and flexibility. In excess, can cause anger or resentment.

Metal Yin 金
or feminine. Associated with determination, strength and rigidity. In excess, can encourage feelings of regret and guilt.

Fire 火
Yang or masculine. Associated with strength and persistence. Brings enthusiasm and creativity. In excess, can cause impatience or aggression.

Water Yin 木
or feminine. Associated with wisdom and intelligence. In excess, can cause a fickle nature.

• • • THE NINE MUSES • • •

In Greek myth, the muses were daughters of Zeus, king of the gods and god of the sky, and Mnemosyne, goddess of the arts and intellectual pursuits. The Greek poet Hesiod was the first to list them, and may have invented their names. It was only in late Roman times that each muse became associated with one particular art, as listed below:

MUSE NAME	ASSOCIATED ART	ADDITIONAL INFORMATION
Calliope	Epic poetry	Mother of Orpheus. Said to be Homer's muse.
Clio	History	Mother of Hyacinth. Beloved of Apollo.
Euterpe	Lyric poetry	Name means "Giver of delight". Usually depicted holding a flute.
Melpomene	Tragedy	Originally the muse of singing. In later times shown wearing tragic mask and *cothernus* boots associated with tragic actors.
Terpsichore	Dance	Also the muse of the chorus, a regular feature of Greek drama. Typically shown plucking at a lyre.
Erato	Love poetry	Also often depicted with a kithara or lyre.
Polyhymnia	Sacred poetry	The muse of hymns to the gods. Later also associated with mime and pantomime.
Urania	Astronomy	Also associated with astrology. Sometimes shown in a cloak decorated with stars.
Thalia	Comedy and bucolic poetry	A rustic figure, shown with a comic mask or shepherd's staff.

• • • *SOLE MAPS* • • •

In reflexology, the feet are considered a microcosm of the body. The toes represent the head area; the outside edges of the soles, the outer edges of the body (shoulders, waist, hips); the inner edges, the spine. To work on a particular area of the body, therefore, you massage a particular area on the feet. Most reflexology points are on the soles, as shown in the diagram below (others are on the hands and ears: *see p84*). The basic principle is to unblock *qi* (life force) within the body's energy system.

The reflexology touch should be firm, with the thumb or finger flexed. Work slowly with the flat pad of your thumb in a "creeping" movement, as if you are pushing pins into a pincushion.

Caution: Do not use reflexology on a pregnant woman or on anyone with a serious health complaint – consult a qualified reflexologist.

RIGHT FOOT   **LEFT FOOT**

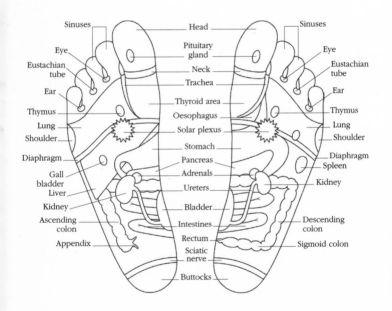

SOLES

• • • *FAIRY SIGNS* • • •

Fairies appear in almost every folklore tradition in the world. Common types include elves, trolls, house spirits (such as brownies in Scotland, *domovoi* in Slavic regions and *tomte* in Scandinavia), and changelings (fairy offspring secretly left in place of human babies, known as *xaninos* in Spain). Among the phenomena that are taken as signs of fairy life are:

Elf-shot
Stone Age flint arrowheads, attributed in Scotland and N England to fairy battles (which were thought to be the cause of ailments in cattle).

Elf-locks
Tangled snarls in children's hair, sometimes said in England to be caused by fairies dancing over them when they sleep (when they're not diving under their pillows to exchange teeth for money!).

Fairy rings
Raised or discoloured circles of grass, or rings of mushrooms, appearing overnight, thought to be the remains of nocturnal fairy dances. Standing inside one was said to bring bad luck, even early death.

Fairy forts
Prehistoric ring-forts, overgrown with vegetation. Some say that they are repositories for leprechaun gold and protected by druidic magic; others that they are portals to the fairy world.

••• ✿ •••

• • • *THREE BODHISATTVAS* • • •

In Theravada Buddhism, a *bodhisattva* is any living being who is sincerely striving toward enlightenment. In the Mahayana tradition, a bodhisattva is a being who has already reached enlightenment but refrains from entering *nirvana* (a state free from suffering and reincarnation), choosing to remain in the realm of *samsara* (life, death, rebirth) to help liberate others. There are said to be three principal bodhisattvas, each of whom embodies a particular virtue. These figures appear extensively in Mahayana iconography:

Majushri: wisdom
Depicted with a flaming sword in his right hand (to destroy ignorance) and a book of supreme wisdom in his left hand. In the Mahayana tradition, believed to be a disciple of the Buddha.

Avalokiteshvara: compassion
Known in at least 108 forms. Sometimes depicted with 1,000 arms, signifying his ability to reach out to people, and 1,000 eyes, suggesting his ability to perceive suffering wherever it occurs. In China, well known in the feminine manifestation, Guan Yin, goddess of mercy.

Vajrapani: power
Depicted dancing in a halo of flames, with a thunderbolt (*vajra*) in his right hand denoting his ability to cut through the darkness of delusion.

• SIX FUNERARY TEXTS OF EGYPT •

From the 3rd millennium BCE, Egyptians of wealth and power had spells inscribed on their coffins, to secure a safe trip through the afterlife. Later these developed into illustrated papyrus scrolls buried with the deceased – the best known in the West being the Egyptian Book of the Dead.

The Amduat
(Book of the Secret Chamber)
Oldest of the royal funerary texts: only pharaohs or highly favoured nobility were allowed to use it. Charts the journey of the sun god through the twelve divisions of the Underworld (corresponding with the hours of the night) and lists the allies and the foes the pharaoh will encounter on the same journey.

The Book of Gates
Again, traces the journey of the soul into the next world, following the path of the sun, but this time describing twelve gates, each associated with a specific goddess, whose character the deceased soul must recognize. Failure to do so will result in punishment in a lake of fire.

The Book of the Dead
(Book of Coming Forth by Day)
Available to all Egyptians, regardless of status. A collection of almost 200 spells, hymns and prayers, which became fully evolved by 1600BCE. Includes vignettes of such ceremonies as the weighing of the heart (it had to be feather-light to qualify for paradise) and the opening of the mouth (restoring bodily functions to the mummy, so it could be used in the afterlife). Having been tested before Osiris, the judge of the dead, and found pure, the soul assumes cosmic power among the gods. It might be invited to travel in the barque of the sun, with millions of others, and wage war against the chaos serpent, Apep. (*See also p90.*)

The Book of Caverns
Less illustrated and more literary than other funerary texts. Each cavern has a challenge that the soul must pass. Gives a graphic view of the torments of hell – beheading, ripping of the soul from the chest, and so on.

The Book of the Heavens
Late New Kingdom texts, including the Book of the Night, the Book of the Day, the Book of Nut and the Book of the Heavenly Cow. They describe the night-time journey of the sun into and through the body of Nut, goddess of the heavens, who gives birth to a rejuvenated sun in the morning.

The Book of the Earth
(Book of Aker or The Creation of the Solar Disc)
Describes how the sun disc was raised from the earth by pairs of arms in the underworld, and the punishment of unblessed souls in the Place of Annihilation. Gives more emphasis to the earth gods Aker, Geb and Tatenen than other texts.

••• ALCHEMY: THE FOUR STAGES •••
OF THE MAGNUM OPUS

The main goal of alchemists was the transmutation of common metals into gold or silver – a metaphor for the transformation of base matter into spirit. To achieve this they sought obsessively for the "philosopher's stone", the agent of transformation. The search for this component was called the Magnum Opus, or "Great Work", and had three main stages:

Nigredo *("Blackening")*  A phase of putrefaction or decomposition, in which ingredients were cleansed and heated to form a homogeneous black matter. In metaphorical terms, this was the torpor from which the soul had to be aroused to achieve spiritual rebirth. Said to last 40 days.

Albedo *("Whitening")* Purging the black matter to remove impurities, using a liquid referred to as *aqua vitae*, the "water of life". A stage known as *citrinitas* ("yellowness") was also sometimes needed: the yellowing of silver into gold. Together, the two processes represented spiritual cleansing, a precursor to psychic transformation.

Rubedo *("Reddening")* The final stage of accomplished transmutation, when the alchemist's work in progress took on the reddish hue of true gold. Legend claimed that the 13th-century chemist and bishop Albertus Magnus achieved this feat, thereby creating the philosopher's stone. Spiritually, this phase represents the fusion of spirit and matter.

••• ✿ •••

••• SHINTO TORII:
GATEWAYS TO THE SACRED

The entrances to Shinto shrines in Japan are traditionally marked by wooden gateways, or *torii*. These symbolize the transition from secular to sacred space (where spirits, or *kami*, reside). Most *torii* have two upright posts, topped by two horizontal bars, the *kasagi* (upper) and *nuki* (lower), and are painted orange-red.

One theory is that *torii* were originally symbolic bird-perches: in Shinto, birds are seen as divine messengers. Some shrines have numerous *torii*, donated by worshippers in devotion or gratitude – the Fushimi Inari Shrine, Kyoto, has thousands, which cover the paths to the inner shrine. There are also "floating *torii*", sited offshore.

• TESTIMONIES OF THE QUAKERS •

The Religious Society of Friends (the Quakers) was established in England in the 17th century, chiefly by the dissenter George Fox. Its central idea is the "Light of Christ Within". Some other cherished values are expressed in a series of "testimonies":

Testimony of Peace: Pacificism is a key belief, inspired by Christ's injunction that we should love our enemies. Many Quaker conscientious objectors have served prison terms during wars. The Society was awarded the Nobel Peace Prize in 1947.

Testimony of Truth (or Integrity): Quakers strive to be true to God, to themselves and to others. From a core of personal integrity flow outward values such as fairness and honesty.

Testimony of Simplicity: Plainness of dress is seen as having moral value: fashion is wasteful and can highlight social inequalities. Plainness of speech (avoiding honorific titles, affirming rather than swearing oaths) is similarly important. "Thee" and "thou" were once favoured as less formal than "you".

Testimony of Equality: As all people have the divine spark inside themselves, equality is God-given. Early Quakers in the USA worked for abolition of slavery, fair treatment of Native Americans, and better conditions in mental facilities. Equality of the sexes has also been promoted: women had separate meetings, but this was designed to foster independence from their husbands.

••• ❀ •••

THE LINEAGE OF SRI T. KRISHNAMACHARYA

Two of the most famous yogis of the modern world are **B.K.S. Iyengar** (b.1918), who founded the disciplined, alignment-focused Iyengar style of yoga, and **K. Patthabi Jois** (b.1915), who pioneered the dynamic, flowing style known as Astanga Vinyasa yoga. Despite being known for their diverse – and some would think opposing – styles, the two men shared a teacher: Sri T. Krishnamacharya (1888–1989).

Tirumalai Krishnamacharya was a scholar of Sanskrit and philosophy, who had spent seven years studying in a cave in the Himalayas with his own guru, before becoming a teacher himself. His teaching style successfully integrated the ancient philosophies of yoga with modern-day requirements. He became renowned in later life for being able to use his yogic skills to stop (and restart) his own heartbeat.

Many of Krishnamacharya's other students also went on to become influential teachers, including his son, **T.K.V. Desikachar** (b.1938), who developed a yoga style that focuses on individual needs and abilities, and **Indra Devi** (1899–2002), who went on to teach worldwide – she was the first Western woman to be taken under Krishnamacharya's tutelage.

• NATIVE AMERICAN TRICKSTERS •

The trickster, a subversive figure who deceives and exploits his fellow creatures for his own gratification but who is also often duped or humbled himself, appears in the myths of most Native American peoples. He was frequently a semi-divine but largely amoral presence at the creation of the world. However coarse and selfish he may have seemed, his mischievous antics more often than not provoked affectionate laughter, while his mythic powers inspired awe.

Raven

For Natives of the NW Coast and the Arctic and subarctic zones, Raven was, and is, a heroic creator, as well as the ultimate trickster. This dichotomy reflected local opinion of the bird of the same name: although viewed as highly intelligent, it was also seen as unpredictable and rather comical.

Hare

Played a similar role to Raven in the mythology of other tribes. In tales of the Winnebago (Nebraska), he was born of a virgin who died, leaving him to be raised by his grandmother, an earth spirit, who had to rescue him from many scrapes. Hare also featured in some African myths and, via the tales told by slaves in America, may have been the inspiration for the Brer Rabbit stories popularized by Joel Chandler Harris.

Coyote

Perhaps the most widespread character in all Native American folklore. Features in several creation myths – for example, kicking a ball of mud until it became the form of the first man. Many of the tales combine admiration for his resourcefulness with contempt for his relentlessly self-serving, scavenging ways. In many stories he ended up exiled or dead, yet he was indestructible, so always returned to embark on new adventures. Still well-known today thanks to his incarnation in cartoon form as Wile E. Coyote.

Nihansan

The spider trickster of the Arapaho tribe (eastern plains of Colorado and Wyoming). One well-known tale describes Nihansan himself being tricked. After a long journey, he spotted some juicy-looking plums on a river-bed and dived in to gather them. After several fruitless underwater forays, he noticed the plums hanging from a tree above his head – he had been diving for mere reflections.

Manabozho

A trickster of the Ojibway people on the US–Canadian border, Manabozho was known for his cunning: he was good at persuading prey to let themselves be killed and eaten. Yet in other tales he was the butt of the joke – in one he asked his own rear end to guard a fowl roasting on a fire, only to set it alight as punishment when he found the bird gone.

••• TEN USES FOR A CLEAR •••
QUARTZ CRYSTAL

Purify water by dropping the crystal into a jug of water and leaving it overnight.

Extend the life of cut flowers by adding it to the water in a vase.

Keep fruit fresh for longer by placing it in your fruit bowl.

Speed up the growth of seeds by placing it near your seed tray.

Counteract the negative effects of electromagnetic fields by placing it near electrical equipment such as TVs and microwaves.

Help to prevent engine trouble by placing it under your car hood.

Boost your concentration at work by placing it somewhere prominent on your desk.

Dispel negativity by carrying it in your pocket.

Soften and brighten your skin by adding it to your bath water ten minutes before climbing in.

Promote good skin tone by holding it (must be wand-shaped) in your right hand over your face and body, point facing but not touching your skin, and making small clockwise circles.

••• ✿ •••

••• THE FOUR TYPES •••
OF QI DISHARMONY

Traditional Chinese medicine is based on the principle that health problems can occur when the *qi* or "vital energy" in your body is out of balance. *Qi* imbalance occurs in four main ways, listed below. It is most commonly treated using a combination of acupuncture and herbs to target specific areas and smooth out the energetic flow.

1. **Deficient qi** (*qi xu*): A low level of *qi* can cause a variety of problems, from pallor, lethargy and insomnia to coughs and tinnitus. Often undermines the ability of elderly people to keep warm.

2. **Sinking qi** (*qi xian*): This more severe *qi* deficiency can prevent the body from holding organs and tissues in place, causing conditions such as uterine prolapse or a collapsed lung.

3. **Stagnant qi** (*qi zhi*): Blocked or sluggish *qi*, possibly caused by stress, trauma or over-indulgence. Can cause headaches, swelling of organs and around joints, oedema, depression, abdominal pain and infertility.

4. **Rebellious qi** (*qi ni*): Qi that is flowing the wrong way. In the stomach, this can lead to hiccups, nausea and vomiting; in the lungs, coughing and wheezing; in the spleen, diarrhoea.

. . . *THE MAGICAL MEANINGS* . . .
OF RUNES

Runes were widely used for writing, divination and magic in early Anglo-Saxon, Germanic and Scandinavian societies, and are still revered today for their sacred symbolism. By combining the appropriate runes in a line on a sheet of paper or parchment (known as a "runescript") you can aim to acquire certain qualities or to make particular outcomes occur. For example, to attract love, you might include Ur (new circumstances), Geofu (harmony) and Wynn (love). Below are the major meanings of the 24 characters in the original runic alphabet (Elder Futhark), to help you to construct your own runescripts.

NAME	SYMBOL	MEANING	NAME	SYMBOL	MEANING
Feoh		Increase in wealth, relationship consolidation	**Yr**		Protection, removal of obstacles
Ur		New circumstances or conditions	**Peorth**		Finding lost things
Thorn		Good luck, protection from own folly	**Eolh**		Protection against evil thoughts
Ansur		Academic success, healthy communication	**Sigel**		Health, strength, self-confidence
Rad		Safe travel	**Tir**		Victory
Ken		Positivity, well-being, fresh starts, stable relationships	**Beorc**		Healthy domestic affairs, birth, children
Geofu		Harmony in partnerships	**Eoh**		Change
Wynn		Fulfilment in love or career	**Mann**		Goodwill, assistance from others
Hagall		Good luck	**Lagu**		Intuition, psychic power
Nied		Patience with long-term goals, success in relationships	**Ing**		Problem-solving, conclusions
Is		Continuity	**Daeg**		Financial gain, resolutions
Jara		Help in legal matters, tangible results	**Othel**		Protection of possessions and investments

... THE PRINCIPAL NORSE ...
GODS AND GODDESSES

The ancient Norse pantheon was split between two rival tribes – the Aesir and the Vanir. The Aesir gods were mostly associated with warfare and the sky, while the Vanir were linked with agriculture and fertility. The two groups eventually fought in a war, which was won by the Aesir. Later they lived together peacefully in the celestial realm of Asgard.

AESIR DEITIES

Odin Chief god of Asgard and supreme Aesir divinity. Formidable warrior, who possessed shape-shifting powers and could foresee the future. Received the souls of half of all dead warriors in the hall of Valhalla (the other half were received by Freyja, see below).

Frigg Wife of Odin. Stately, gracious, maternal, as shown in the myth of her son Balder, when she ordered his brother to rescue him from the dead. Invoked by women in childbirth or wishing to conceive.

Thor Eldest son of Odin. Mighty figure of colossal strength – god of thunder, ruler of the sky and protector of Asgard. Spent much of his time battling his enemies, the giants.

Sif Wife of Thor. Beautiful goddess, whose golden hair was cut off by the trickster Loki and replaced by a headpiece made by dwarves.

Balder Son of Odin and Frigg. Associated with light, virtue and beauty. Killed with mistletoe spear made by Loki, and mourned by all the gods.

Forseti Son of Balder. God of justice. Settled legal disputes.

Tyr God of combat, generally depicted as one-handed, the other hand having been bitten off by the wolf Fenrir. Venerated by warriors.

VANIR DEITIES

Njord God of the sea and patriarch of the Vanir line. Toasts were often offered to him and his son Freyr to secure peace and prosperity.

Freyr Son of Njord. Principal god of agriculture, regulating sun and rain. Also associated with sexual procreation.

Freyja Daughter of Njord. Goddess of love and fertility. Also associated with battle and death – received the souls of half of all dead warriors in the hall of Fólkvangr (the other half were received by Odin).

Loki Trickster of Asgard. Troublemaker with shape-shifting powers. Punished for his role in Balder's death by being tied up with his own son's intestines. Destined to break free at Ragnarok, the end of the current age, when he will fight alongside the giants against the gods.

• THEORIES OF THE UNCONSCIOUS •

Psychologists **Sigmund Freud** (1856–1939) and **Carl Jung** (1875–1961) are both well-known for the advances they made in exploring the workings of the unconscious mind in the early 20th century.

Freud's major contribution was to devise a three-tier structure for the human psyche. He claimed that all mental life could be described in terms of the activity within, and the interaction between, three levels:

Id: Entirely unconscious element present from birth, responsible for basic urges such as hunger and sex. Instinctual, egocentric and amoral. Ruled by the pleasure–pain principle.	***Ego:*** Aspect evolving from the *id*, responsible for reason and common sense. Operates unconsciously and consciously to balance primitive drives and social demands.	***Superego:*** The most evolved aspect. Acts mainly unconsciously, as a moral compass and conscience, policing the drives of the *id*. Comprises personal ideals and spiritual goals.

Jung's major contribution, which he saw as supplementing the Freudian model, was the concept of the ***collective unconscious:*** an innate fund of experience held in common by all, which expresses itself in the archetypal symbols that appear in dreams, visions and intuitions (*see p114*). Like the cave in Jung's dream of the house (*see p46*), this layer of mental activity underlies all other layers (both conscious and unconscious): a psychic substratum linking all of humankind.

••• 🏵 •••

• THE GHOST HUNTER'S TOOL KIT •

"Scientific" ghost hunting was pioneered in the 1930s by British journalist and psychical researcher **Harry Price** (1881–1948) (*see also p19*). The list below is based on the items that Price took with him to help with his investigations:

Soft felt overshoes To keep as silent as possible when moving around a haunted site.

Notebook and pen To record the details of any strange occurrences as soon as they happen.

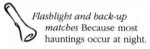

Flashlight and back-up matches Because most hauntings occur at night.

Non-permanent marker To mark spots where strange events occur.

Camera with flash To gain photographic evidence and bolster the credibility of the episode.

First-aid kit In case of accidents.

Cassette or other sound recorder To capture any strange noises.

Bowl of mercury To detect tremors – a phenomenon associated with poltergeist manifestations.

THE NINE MYTHICAL EMPERORS OF ANCIENT CHINA

Seeking to impose order on China's many myths, ancient scholars in the centuries following Confucius (551–579BCE) constructed a legendary early history, which tracked the transfer of power through nine mythical rulers.

The first three emperors, often referred to collectively as the Three Sovereigns, were supernatural beings linked with the gods, while the last three, known as the Sage Kings, were fully human, eulogized by Confucius as models for subsequent rulers. Between them, these nine rulers are said to have bestowed the arts of civilization on the Chinese people:

Fuxi (c.2900BCE)
Known as *Tao Hao* ("Great Brilliance"). A divine being with a serpent's body. Brother and husband of the creator goddess Nuwa – from their union the human race was born. Introduced hunting, cooking, fishing with nets, and the trigrams of the *I Ching* (*see p12*).

↓

Shennong (c.2800BCE)
Known as *Yandi* ("Fiery Emperor"). A divine being with a bird's head. Encouraged people to clear land to grow crops, and introduced the cart and plough. Also regarded as the father of Chinese medicine, trying out hundreds of herbal recipes on himself.

↓

Huangdi (c.2700BCE)
The "Yellow Emperor". Established the principles of Chinese medicine, which helped him to live to be more than 100 years old. Wise ruler and great warrior. Established unity and stability among warring tribes. Introduced houses and boats, bows and arrows, silk-weaving and the art of writing. Redistributed land. On his death he is supposed to have climbed to heaven to become the king of the gods.

↓

Shaohao (c.2600BCE)
Son of Huangdi. Introduced the 25-string lute. A pyramid-shaped structure in Shandong province is said to be his tomb.

↓

Zhuanxu (c.2500BCE)
Nephew of Shaohao and grandson of Huangdi. Religious reformer who discouraged shamanism. Made contributions to a unified calendar and replaced the matriarchal system with a patriarchal one.

↓

Kudi (c.2400BCE)
Cousin of Zhuanxu. Encouraged musical composition and ordered the musician You Chui to develop new instruments. Also promoted education, setting up schools.

↓

Yao (c.2300BCE)

Son of Kudi. Model ruler who lived frugally and cared for his people.
Summoned the divine archer Yi to help when ten suns rose over
his drought-prone kingdom. Chose a hard-working farmer, Shun, as
his successor over his own "unworthy" son.

↓

Shun (c.2300BCE)

Earned his position through merit, a model ruler. Standardized weights
and measures, regulated rivers and divided China into twelve provinces.

↓

Yu the Great (c.2200BCE)

Known as the Flood-Tamer for his many hydrological projects,
achieved with the help of dragons. Founder of the Xia Dynasty, the
first dynasty listed in historical records (although firm evidence of it
has yet to be found).

• • • *NUMBER SYMBOLISM* • • •

Numbers, being abstracted from the world of forms, readily acquire
mystic significance. Here are common associations with the digits 1 to 9:

1 The sun, the one God, beginnings, creation, pure energy, positivity, solo endeavour, will, action, unity, the phallus (masculinity), power.

2 The moon, balance, duality, judgment, partnership, union, choice, intuition.

3 Jupiter, the Trinity (unity in diversity), magic, intuition, fertility, new ventures, harmony, proportion, the Masonic triangle; past, present and future; birth, life and death.

4 Uranus, the square, the cross, wholeness, completion, stability, groundedness, solidity, roots, the seasons, the elements, the cardinal points.

5 Mercury, the pentagram, humankind, will, change, travel, adventure, movement, freedom, instability, unpredictability, rebellion.

6 Venus, harmony, balance, love, truth, enlightenment, compassion, forgiveness.

7 Neptune, the macrocosm and microcosm, days of the week, deadly sins, stages of man, magic, esotericism, imagination, dreaming, knowledge.

8 Saturn, business, success, wealth, repetition, cycles, continuation, determination.

9 Mars, invention, influence, attainment, accomplishment, satisfaction, pain, sadness.

• • • THE HIERARCHY OF ANGELS • • •

Classifying angels was a popular academic pastime of the Middle Ages. One of the most influential hierarchies was that proposed by 5th-century theologian and philosopher Pseudo-Dionysius the Areopagite. In his text *The Celestial Hierarchy,* he categorized angels into nine orders, or "choirs", divided across three triads, or "spheres":

FIRST SPHERE **Guardians of God's throne**	SECOND SPHERE **Governors of the heavens**	THIRD SPHERE **Heavenly messengers**
Seraphim: Angels closest to God, who perpetually praise Him. So dazzling that even other divine beings can't look upon them.	*Dominions:* Regulators of the duties of "lower" angels in line with God's wishes.	*Principalities:* Sources of blessings and much inspiration on Earth.
Cherubim: All-knowing protectors of light, the stars and God's glory.	*Virtues:* Supervisors of the movement of the heavenly bodies, ensuring the orderly running of the universe.	*Archangels:* "Highest" form of angel with whom most humans come into contact. They oversee the angels (below).
Thrones: Voices of divine authority. They mirror God's goodness by seeking justice for all.	*Powers:* Recorders of eternal history and overseers of the distribution of power among humans.	*Angels:* Messengers to the earthly realm, commonly featuring in human visions or premonitions.

• • • THE FOUR NOBLE TRUTHS • • •

Buddhism teaches that in order to achieve freedom from *samsara* (the cycle of life, death and rebirth) we must accept the Four Noble Truths – a diagnosis of, and prescribed treatment for, the human condition:

1. ***The nature of suffering (dukkha):*** Life inevitably involves suffering, both physical and emotional. Nothing is permanent.

2. ***The origin of suffering (samudaya):*** At the root of all suffering is our attachment to desire – for pleasure, for happiness.

3. ***The cessation of suffering (nirodha):*** We can end our suffering by non-attachment – by freeing ourselves from desire.

4. ***The path (marga) to the cessation of suffering:*** We can rid ourselves of desire by the Noble Eightfold Path (Right Wisdom, Morality and Concentration: *see p71*). Thus we can gain nirvana.

• • FIVE EGYPTIAN PYRAMIDS • •

Built as tombs for the pharaohs, pyramids are the most prominent and lasting symbols of ancient Egyptian civilization. The best-known surviving examples are:

Step Pyramid of Djoser

Built c.2630BCE for a 3rd-Dynasty pharaoh, named Djoser. 203ft (62m) high. Located in the Saqqar necropolis. The tallest building of its time, and thought to be the first pyramid tomb ever constructed. Formed of six stacked *mastabas* (the rectangular tombs in which pharaohs were buried before pyramids), each one smaller than the one below.

Great Pyramid of Khufu

Built c.2570BCE for the second of the 4th-Dynasty pharaohs, Khufu (son of Sneferu). 481ft (146.6m) high. Located in the Giza necropolis, on the outskirts of Cairo. Sits alongside two other pyramids (Khafre and Menkaure), as well as the statue of the Great Sphinx. The world's tallest structure for over 3,800 years, and the only one of the Seven Wonders of the Ancient World still in existence today.

Bent Pyramid of Sneferu

Built c.2600BCE for the first of the 4th-Dynasty pharaohs, Sneferu. 344ft (105m) high. Located in the Dahshur necropolis. The first smooth-sided (as opposed to stepped) pyramid. Its lower section is at 55° while its upper section is at 43° – thought to be the result of structural issues encountered during the pyramid's construction.

Pyramid of Khafre

Built c.2530BCE for the fourth of the 4th-Dynasty pharaohs, Khafr (son of Khufu). 471ft (143.5m) high. Located in Giza. The second tallest of the three pyramids, but sits on a 10m (33ft) thick bedrock, making it appear taller. Smaller at the base than the Great Pyramid, and rises at a steeper angle.

Pyramid of Neferirkare

Built c.2460BCE for a 5th-Dynasty pharaoh, Neferirkare Kakai; unfinished at the time of his death. 236ft (72m) high. Located in the Abusir necropolis, tallest of the pyramids there. Built on the area's highest point. Originally a step pyramid but later filled to give it a true, smooth-sided pyramidal shape.

... *THREE MUDRAS FROM THE* ...
LIFE OF THE BUDDHA

A *mudra* is a symbolic hand gesture, of the kind used in meditation.

No Fear	**Earth-touching**	**The wheel's turning**
The Buddha, attacked by the elephant Nalagiri, used the "No fear" or *Abhaya mudra* to calm the animal, before passing on the *dharma* ("teachings") to him.	After reaching enlightenment under the bodhi tree, the Buddha touched the earth with his right hand so that it bore witness to the episode. This is the "Earth-touching" or *Bhumisparsa mudra*.	After enlightenment, the Buddha taught the *dharma* to monks in the deer park. As he did so, he adopted the *Dharmachakra mudra*, representing the "turning of the wheel of the dharma" (*see p 71*).

••• ✦ •••

• *IMPORTANT ISLAMIC FESTIVALS* •

Most Islamic festivals commemorate events that relate to the life of the prophet Mohammed (c.570–632CE). Dates for these are fixed in the Muslim, or Hijri, calendar (354 days in a year, split across twelve lunar months). These are the most significant:

DURING MONTH 1 – MUHARRAM
Day 1: *Al-hijra*, the Islamic New Year, commemorates Mohammed's journey from Mecca to Medina, c.622CE (the *hijra*).
Day 10: *Ashura* marks the death of Imam Hussein (Mohammed's grandson) at the Battle of Karbala, for Shi'ite Muslims.

DURING MONTH 3 – RABI' I
Day 12: *Mawlid* celebrates Mohammed's birthday.

DURING MONTH 9 – RAMADAN
(*holiest month, involving daily fasting from dawn to dusk*)
Day 27: *Laylat al-Qadr* marks the revelation of the first verses of the Qur'an to Mohammed by the Angel Jibril (Gabriel).

DURING MONTH 10 – SHAWWAL
Day 1: *Eid al-Fitr* celebrates the end of Ramadan and the breaking of the fast.

DURING MONTH 12 – DHU AL-HIJJA
(*month of the* hajj *– the great pilgrimage to Mecca*)
Day 9: *Yawm 'Arafat* recalls the farewell sermon given by Mohammed on his *hajj*.
Day 10: *Eid al-Adha* marks the end of the *hajj* and commemorates God giving Abraham a sacrificial ram to prevent the death of his son.

✛══✳══✛

• • • FOUR APOCRYPHAL GOSPELS • • •

Apocrypha means "hidden things" in Greek. The apocryphal books of Christianity are texts not generally included in the biblical "canon" (the authorized scriptures), often because their date, authorship or authenticity is uncertain. However, they were favoured by the Gnostics and other sects. Many apocryphal gospels were discovered in the late 19th and early 20th centuries. Some, such as the books of Enoch, Judith, Tobit and Esther, relate to the Old Testament; others, such as the four gospels listed below that were found in Egypt, relate to the New Testament.

The Gospel of Thomas
The non-narrative writings of the apostle Thomas (also known as Doubting Thomas owing to his initial unwillingness to accept Jesus' resurrection). A series of *logia* (dialogues and sayings) attributed to Jesus. Dates back to c.200CE.

The Gospel of Mary
A fragment of text that gives insight into the relationship between Jesus, the apostles and Mary Magdalene. Has been used to support the legitimacy of women's spiritual leadership. Dates back to the 2nd century CE.

The Gospel of Philip
A collection of teachings famous for suggesting that Jesus was married to Mary Magdalene (she is described as his "lover" in some translations). Dates back to c.300CE.

The Gospel of Judas
A text documenting conversations between Judas Iscariot and Jesus. Portrays Judas as obeying Christ's instructions, rather than betraying him as depicted in the Bible. Dates back to c.280CE.

••• ❀ •••

• • • A BRIEF HISTORY OF REIKI • • •

Reiki is a Japanese healing technique that involves a practitioner placing his or her hands on, or above, a patient's body in specific positions in order to channel the life force (universal energy, or *ki*) into it.

The practice is believed to date back to the end of the 19th century when a Japanese doctor, **Mikao Usui** (1865–1926), began a quest to rediscover a universal energy that could be used for healing, irrespective of the practitioner's mental or physical state. Fasting and meditating for 21 days on Mount Kuriyama, he received the gift of Reiki.

He went on to develop "The Usui System of Natural Healing", including the Reiki Ideals, the Reiki symbols (*see p84*), the hand positions and the attunement process. He trained many others in his methods. Since then, the original Usui method has been modified in numerous ways by different followers, and today there are at least 30 variations of the original Reiki system.

✦✦✦

• • • *SUN SALUTATION* • • •

Sun Salutation, or *Surya Namaskar* in Sanskrit, is a series of flowing yoga postures performed according to the rhythm of your breath: you inhale each time you lengthen the body, and exhale each time you contract it. The sequence works many of the body's main muscles and effectively distributes *prana* (*see p104*) throughout your system. It is often done at the start and/or end of a full yoga session but can also be used as a short practice in itself. There are a number of Sun Salutation variations: the cycle shown below is just one option. A full "round" involves doing this cycle twice – the first time stepping backward on the right foot for the lunge in posture 4 and forward on the same (right) foot in posture 9; the second time stepping backward on the left foot in posture 4 and forward on the same (left) foot in posture 9.

1. Mountain Pose 2. Upward arm stretch 3. Standing Forward Bend
4. Backward Lunge 5. Plank Pose 6. Half Four-limbed Staff Pose
7. Upward-facing Dog 8. Downward-facing Dog 9. Opposite Lunge
10. Standing Forward Bend 11. Upward arm stretch 12. Mountain Pose

• *THE WHO'S WHO OF TRANSLUCENCE* •

The great spiritual texts describe important awakenings – from St Paul on the road to Damascus, to the Buddha under the bodhi tree. Modern author and teacher Arjuna Ardagh believes we are on the brink of a *mass* spiritual awakening or "translucence". He claims that around 4 million people worldwide have already experienced translucence – including well-known New Age seekers and gurus. These include:

Eckhart Tolle
(b.1948): Had a profound spiritual awakening at the age of 29. His books, including the *The Power of Now*, emphasize practising meditation to help us live in the moment.

Byron Katie
(b.1942): Author of several books, including *Loving What Is*. Founder of a process of self-inquiry – "The Work". She teaches that opening our minds can set us free.

Neale Donald Walsch *(b.1943):* Former advertising executive who wrote a letter to God and "heard back" via automatic writing, forming the basis for his book *Conversations with God* and its sequels. He teaches that all experience, positive or negative, is part of the wonder of life.

Andrew Harvey *(b.1952):* Mystic who studied Hinduism, Buddhism, Christianity and Sufism. Author of *The Direct Path* and *The Sun at Midnight*. He places great importance on the feminine manifestation of God.

Dan Millman *(b.1946):* Former Olympic gymnast and author of *The Way of the Peaceful Warrior*. He believes that every moment deserves our complete attention.

Thomas Moore *(c.1940):* Former Catholic monk and psychotherapist. Author of several books, including *Care of the Soul*. He stresses the importance of recognizing the spirituality of everyday moments.

Marianne Williamson *(b.1952):* Author of several books, including *A Return to Love*. She teaches the power of love to overcome fear and transform one's life.

• • *THE THREE BASKETS* • •

After his death the Buddha left a body of oral teachings that was gathered together in three distinct groups for the benefit of future generations: the so-called *Tipitaka* ("three baskets"). The only complete *Tipitaka* collection is that of the Theravada school, preserved as the "Pali canon". Its three components are as follows:

• *Sutra Pitaka* – discourses attributed to the Buddha and his followers.
• *Vinaya Pitaka* – guidelines relating to the rules of monastic discipline.
• *Abhidharma Pitaka* – analytical texts, describing how the world seemed from the perspective of one who had gained enlightenment.

• • HEALTH-GIVING HERBAL TEAS • •

These herbal teas offer a wide range of healing benefits. To make an infusion, pour some freshly boiled water over a sachet or loose ingredients in a small teapot or cup, and leave to steep for 4–5 minutes.

Burdock
Anti-inflammatory, cleanses the blood, boosts the liver

Cardamom
Stimulates digestion, eases stomach cramps

Chamomile
Calms nerves, induces sleep

Cinnamon
Alleviates common colds, warming, improves circulation

Dandelion
Diuretic, cleanses the liver

Fennel
Improves appetite, aids digestion, soothes sore throats

Ginger
Boosts circulation, relieves cold and flu, eases digestion

Lemon Balm
Relaxes nerves, soothes digestion

Liquorice
Reduces allergies, eases menstrual cramps

Mint
Calms digestion, relieves headaches

Nettle
Cleanses the blood, improves kidney and liver functions

Raspberry Leaf
Antioxidant, relieves menstrual tension

Rosehip
Soothes headaches and bladder infections

Sage
Calms nerves, alleviates lung congestion and relieves coughs

Valerian
Promotes sleep, eases stomach cramps

Caution: If you have any health conditions, are on medication, or are pregnant or breast-feeding, check with your health practitioner before drinking herbal teas.

• THE TWELVE MAJOR MERIDIANS •

In the Chinese healing tradition, meridians are channels in the body through which *qi* (vital energy) travels. To achieve optimum health, your *qi* must flow smoothly. There are twelve major meridians, each corresponding to a different organ (see below). Six meridians are yang (warm, active), six yin (still, passive). Each has a number of "pressure points", through which energy can be channelled and regulated. Having these "needled" through acupuncture can balance unharmonious *qi* (*see p56*) and boost vitality.

Yang meridians	Yin meridians
lung	large intestine
heart	small intestine
liver	gall bladder
kidney	bladder
spleen	stomach
triple heater (*sanjiao*)	heart governor (pericardium)

• THE THREE NORSE WORLDS •

Ancient Norse mythology describes a world divided into three main levels, one above the other – connected by the World Tree, Yggdrasil:

Asgard

Realm of the gods (*see also p58*). From here, Odin presided over the whole world, with the aid of his raven spies, Hugin and Munin. Within this realm was Valhalla, one of Odin's great halls, where warriors who died in battle spent the afterlife feasting with the gods.

Midgard

Realm of humans (and giants). Created by Odin from the body of Ymir – a mighty frost-giant and the first living being. Surrounded by a vast ocean in which the huge sea serpent Jörmungandr lived. Connected to Asgard by a flaming bridge called Bifrost, which appeared to mortals as a rainbow.

Niflheim

Realm of the dead. Cold, dark and misty. Ruled over by a half-woman, half-corpse called Hel. People who died as a result of accidents, sickness or old age ended up here. Also home to the corpse-eating serpent-monster Nidhogg, who loved to gnaw at the roots of Yggdrasil, threatening its continued existence (*see also p97*).

• HEROES OF THE TROJAN WAR •

The Trojan war, as depicted in Homer's epics, is one of classical Greece's defining myths. The main heroes of the warring armies are as follows:

The Greeks

Menelaus: King of Sparta. Husband of Helen. His demand for justice after Paris's elopement to Troy with his wife was the direct cause of the war.

Agamemnon: Brother of Menelaus. King of Mycenae. When his envoys failed to bring Helen back from Troy, he sent out a call to arms.

Odysseus: King of the island of Ithaca. Celebrated for his cunning and intelligence, he devised the plan for the Trojan Horse, which finally ended the siege of Troy.

Diomedes: Brave warrior who had also been in love with Helen. Trusted companion of Odysseus.

Nestor: King of Pylos. Old, wise ruler whose counsel was prized above that of all others.

Achilles: Immersed as an infant in the River Styx by his mother, Thetis, making his body invulnerable except for the heel by which she held him. Defeated every warrior he faced but was killed when a poisoned arrow (shot by Paris) struck his heel.

Ajax: Feared fighter. Enraged at not receiving Achilles' armour after his death (a symbol of bravery), he became violently deranged. Then he felt so ashamed, he took his own life.

Philoctetes: Celebrated archer. Shot down Paris in battle.

The Trojans and their allies

Priam: King of Troy. Father of 50 sons. Too old to fight, he witnessed the loss of those dearest to him before himself being killed by Achilles' son, Neoptolemus.

Hector: Eldest son of Priam. Troy's finest warrior. Proposed that Menelaus and Paris settle their differences in single combat. Forced to fight, he led the armies bravely. He was slain in single combat by Achilles.

Paris: Son of Priam. Caused the war by seducing Helen and taking her to Troy. His arrow, guided by the god Apollo, killed Achilles.

Aeneas: Brave warrior. One of the few Trojans to escape after witnessing the murder of King Priam. The god Poseidon prophesied he would one day rule a new Troy – a story taken up by Virgil in the *Aeneid*.

Memnon: King of the Ethiopians. Son of Eos, goddess of the dawn. Reputedly the most beautiful man in the world. Defeated many Greek warriors but was killed in single combat by Achilles.

Penthesilea: Queen of the Amazons. Fearsome warrior. Killed by Achilles, who was so struck by her beauty that he also slew a Greek who jeered at her.

Rhesus: King of Thrace. Famed for his magnificent horses. Killed by Diomedes who, with Odysseus, then stole Rhesus's horses.

. . . *THE FIVE STAGES OF* . . .
THE MYSTICAL PATH

Evelyn Underhill (1875–1941) was an Anglo-Catholic mystic who had her first spiritual encounters as a child. She described them as "abrupt experiences of the peaceful, undifferentiated plane of reality". She wrote extensively on the subject and, in her 1955 book *Mysticism*, defined the five psychological stages of the "mystical path", explaining how they vary between ecstasy and anguish.

1. *Awakening of the Self to Consciousness of Divine Reality*
Usually a sudden, clearly defined experience, characterized by complete joy and wonder.

2. *Purgation of the Self*
An attempt to rid oneself of the imperfections and material desires that stand in the way of union with the Divine. Usually involves intense discipline.

3. *Illumination*
A blissful *awareness* of the Divine but still no true union. Often experienced during meditation or contemplation, and by artists in creative moments.

4. *Purification of the Self*
Also known as the "Dark Night of the Soul". An *attempt* at total surrender – of the self, of personal identity and of will – to the Divine. However, this inevitably fails, causing confusion and despair at the seemingly acute *absence* of the Divine.

5. *Union with the One*
A sense of eternal surrender to, and harmony with, the transcendent order, or divine reality. Results in what Underhill called "divine fecundity". (Eastern and Sufi mystics teach of a still higher stage: total re-absorption of the soul into the Infinite.)

••• ✿ •••

. . . *TURNING THE WHEEL* . . .
OF DHARMA

After the Buddha's enlightenment, he gave his first sermon in a deer park at Sarnath, near Benares (Varanasi). Here, he passed on his teachings, the *dharma*, to just five monks. A well-known symbol for these teachings is the *dharmachakra*, or "wheel of dharma" (see left), which he is said to have "set in motion" that day, beginning the dissemination of his message throughout the world.

The eight spokes of the wheel symbolize the "Noble Eightfold Path" – a key part of his teachings, which followers should aim to put into practice every day, to help them on the path to self-liberation:

Right view
Right intention
Right speech
Right action
Right livelihood
Right effort
Right mindfulness
Right concentration

• • THE LANGUAGE OF FLOWERS • •

Lady Mary Wortley Montague (1689–1762), wife of the English Ambassador to Turkey, observed the Turkish custom of choosing flowers for their symbolic value at the sultan's court, and introduced it to the West. By Victorian times, flowers could deliver a covert message in an intelligible code:

Amaryllis: splendid beauty, pride
Carnation (yellow): disdain, rejection
Carnation (pink): lasting love, loyalty
Carnation (red): admiration, longing
Chrysanthemum (yellow): slighted love
Chrysanthemum (red): sincere love

Chrysanthemum (white): truth
Forget-me-not: true love
Freesia: friendship
Honeysuckle: devoted affection
Ivy: fidelity
Mimosa: secret love
Peony: bashfulness
Rose (red): eternal love
Rose (white): truth
Rose (white with pink blush): devotion, fidelity

• • • ❀ • • •

• THE SYMBOLISM OF THE MENORAH •

The seven-branched candlestick, or menorah, features on Israel's coat of arms, alongside two olive branches. An ancient Jewish symbol, the menorah is said to be a reminder of the miraculous "burning bush" seen by Moses. The candlestick was used in the Temple in Jerusalem. Its branches also relate to the symbolism of the Kabbalistic Tree of Life (*see p113*). Traditionally, a menorah is made from a single piece of metal to symbolize the unity of the divine world. Instructions on its design are given in Exodus 25: 31–40.

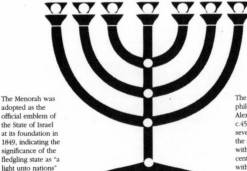

The Menorah was adopted as the official emblem of the State of Israel at its foundation in 1849, indicating the significance of the fledgling state as "a light unto nations" (Isaiah 42: 6).

The Jewish philosopher Philo of Alexandria (c.15BCE–c.45CE) linked the seven branches with the seven "planets", with the sun at the centre; and also with the seven days of creation.

• HOW TO PERFORM SPACE-CLEARING •

Sometimes regarded as a branch of feng shui, space-clearing is the spiritual equivalent of spring cleaning – clearing the home of unwanted negative energy. In its modern form, space-clearing tends to be based on Balinese and Native American traditions. Here's how to do it:

1. Choose an area in your home to cleanse, and open a window so that the "bad" energy can escape. Remove footwear and jewelry. If you hold any spiritual beliefs, pray or humbly ask for help in your ritual.

2. Light an incense stick or smudge stick (*see pp94–5*) and walk around your chosen space, sending smoke into every corner.

3. "Clap" out any negativity by moving slowly around the area, clapping your hands in every corner. Start clapping at the bottom of the wall, then move up toward the ceiling, as high as you can reach. Repeat several times until the clapping sound becomes clear (it will be muffled while the air is still "dirty"). When you've finished, wash your hands.

4. Now make a second circuit, ringing a bell or shaking a rattle into each corner, to balance the energy. If the sound seems "dead" in any spot, continue until it becomes clear.

5. When finished, stamp your feet to re-ground yourself. You may also wish to take a shower and have something to eat or drink.

Caution: Do not perform this if you're menstruating, pregnant or feeling unwell.

• • • THE TRIPLE GODDESS • • •

Cave paintings and prehistoric carvings far more commonly depict women than men – an indication that the female form was considered sacred. Traditions centring on goddess worship have been traced back to 9000BCE in Europe and the Middle East. These goddesses were, and still are, often thought to have three aspects – an important principle for Wiccans, whose main female deity is called the Triple Goddess:

ASPECTS OF THE TRIPLE GODDESS	ATTRIBUTES	MANIFESTATIONS IN OTHER CULTURES	ASSOCIATED COLOUR
MAIDEN: virgin, huntress, the new moon	Innocence, youth, new beginnings, seduction	Persephone, Brigid, Nimue, Kore, Blodeuwedd	White
MOTHER: child-bearer, protector, the full moon	Fertility, birth, ripeness, power, stability, fulfilment	Demeter, Ishtar, Isis, Danu, Hathor, Lakshmi	Red
CRONE: wise guardian, teacher, the waning moon	Compassion, wisdom, experience, death, rebirth	Hecate, Sedna, Baba Yaga, Cailleach, Hel, Hecate	Black

✦ ✦ ✦

• NINE HYBRID MYTHICAL BEASTS •

Common in a wide range of mythologies, hybrid creatures often represented a coming-together of the qualities of their constituent animals. Below is a range of some of the best-known:

Basilisk (Greek)

Part-cockerel, part-serpent. Its breath and gaze were fatal to humans. The best way to kill one was to reflect its own gaze back on it with a mirror. Represented sin in the Christian tradition.

Centaur (Greek)

Half-horse, half-man. Generally symbolized the bestial, uncivilized side of human behaviour – drunk, wild and violent. However, some, such as Chiron, were wise healers and teachers.

Chimera (Greek)

Part-lioness, part-serpent, part-goat. Killed by Bellerophon, who was mounted on the winged horse Pegasus. Symbol of evil in the Christian tradition. An omen of disaster when sighted.

Griffin (Western Asian/Greek)

Part-lion, part-eagle. An especially powerful creature, as the lion was considered king of the beasts and the eagle king of the birds. Guardian of treasure. Symbolized evil in the Christian tradition.

Harpy (Greek)

Part-woman, part-bird. Foul-smelling. Snatched food, objects and people with her sharp talons. Brought pestilence. However, could also be an agent of justice.

Mermaid (many cultures, including Celtic, Japanese, Scandinavian and Polynesian)

Half-woman, half-fish. Symbolized female beauty, vanity and faithlessness. Psychologically, can depict the anima and the deep unconscious (*see p114*).

Satyr (Greek)

Half-man, half-goat. Follower of Bacchus (or in Roman tradition Dionysus), the god of ecstasy and wine. Had a fondness for unrestrained revelry. Symbolized the licentious side of human behaviour.

Simurgh (Persian)

Part-griffin, part-lion, part-peacock, part-snake (although in some myths, it was made up of 30 species of bird). Represented the union between earth and sky, serving as a medium between the two realms. Benevolent, and could save or bestow life.

Sphinx *(Egyptian/Greek)*
Part-human (usually female), part-bull, part-lion
and part-eagle, occasionally depicted with a
bird's or ram's head. Represented the
four elements and regarded as all-wise.
Sphinxes were also viewed as good
temple guardians.

• TAOISM'S EIGHT IMMORTALS •

The secret of eternal life preoccupied Chinese thinkers from the earliest times, and Taoist sages taught that those who achieved perfect union with *qi*, life's essence, could achieve immortality. Stories of the eight mythical individuals listed below, who hailed from a wide variety of backgrounds and had all attained this goal, popularized the idea that immortality was within the grasp of anyone who had the motivation and willpower to attain it.

Li Tieguai
Cripple, with a crutch. Resisted the pleasures of the flesh when tempted with them. Was rewarded with immortality.

Zhongli Quan
Soldier and man of action. Retreated to the mountains on his retirement. While meditating in a cave, a wall opened to reveal a casket that contained the secrets of immortality.

Lan Caihe
Street musician of uncertain gender and age. Used songs to attack the vanity of life and its pleasures. Was wafted to the land of the immortals after passing out drunk in a tavern.

Zhang Guolao
Hermit who was called to the imperial court in his old age. He died on entering the capital but later reappeared in the mountains. Claimed he had served Emperor Yao 3,000 years earlier.

He Xiangu
The only female immortal. Instructed by a spirit to eat some mother-of-pearl and take a vow of chastity, she subsequently lost the need to eat. Was called to the imperial court but disappeared en route, having achieved immortality.

Lu Dongbin
Born into a family of high officials. Dreamed one night of rising to high office, only to be disgraced by unjust accusations. Waking, he saw the vanity of his ambitions and went to be taught by Zhongli Quan instead.

Han Xiang
Scholar, studied under statesman and poet Han Yu. Came to exceed him in magical abilities, such as the power to produce blossoms from a clod of earth. Achieved immortality with the help of Lu Dongbin.

Cao Guojiu
Uncle of an emperor. Escaped execution for involvement in a murder. Moved to the mountains to meditate. Welcomed by Zhongli Quan and Lu Dongbin.

━━ ✳ ━━

• THE BIRTH OF HOMEOPATHY •

Saxony-born **Samuel Hahnemann** (1755–1843) qualified as a doctor in 1791. He soon became disillusioned with the draconian practices of the orthodox medicine of his time, such as blood-letting and purging, and started searching for a gentler, more effective way to cure disease.

Having become acquainted with a book by Dr Edward Cullen, which claimed that quinine was an effective treatment for malaria, Hahnemann developed an interest in cinchona bark (from which quinine is derived), also known as Peruvian bark. He started testing small doses on himself and his friends, and found that it produced, in a healthy person, the symptoms of malaria – the very disease it was said to cure.

He experimented with other known effective cures for various illnesses and found the same effect each time. "In order to cure disease, we must seek medicines that can excite similar symptoms in the healthy body," he wrote, in 1796. *Similiar similibus curentur* – meaning "let like be cured with like" – became the first law of the system of medicine that he coined as "homeopathy" (from the Greek *homois* meaning similar and *pathos* meaning disease or suffering). He, in turn, labelled orthodox medicine "allopathy" or "opposite suffering".

His next step was to dilute his medicines in order to lessen their side-effects. However, he found that this also caused their healing effects to vanish. So he used a technique called "succussion" (shaking the remedy) after dilution, to release the energy of the substance, finding that this increased its healing effects.

••• ✿ •••

• THE YOGA SUTRAS OF PATANJALI •

The key texts of yoga philosophy are the *Yoga Sutras*, written by the renowned Indian sage Patanjali between the 1st and 3rd centuries CE. His *sutras* (or "threads" of wisdom) focus on the workings of the human mind, offering suggestions for practice and behaviour intended to improve quality of life. They consist of 195 short statements in Sanskrit, presented in four chapters:

The first chapter (*Samadhi pada*)
Explains the goal of yoga: a state of attentive contemplation.

The second chapter (*Sadhana pada*)
Presents various methods that will help us to attain this state.

The third and fourth chapters (*Vibhuti pada* and *kaivalya pada*)
Give insight into the extraordinary powers that the contemplative state of yoga can offer us.

> **"Yoga is the stilling of the mind."**
> Yoga Sutras, I.ii

• HOME PILATES: THE MEXICAN WAVE •

This Pilates foot exercise teaches control, improves balance and makes you feel grounded and strong (*see also p112*). It is difficult to do at first, so practise frequently and with patience. If necessary, use your hands initially to isolate the toes, moving them one by one. But also keep trying now and then to move the toes independently.

step 1:
Stand with your feet shoulder-width apart. Feel the bones of your feet (the metatarsals) flat on the floor. During the rest of the exercise, your feet should not roll from side to side, nor should your heels come off the floor.

step 2:
Separate out the toes of your right foot and lift them off the floor one at a time, starting with the big toe (like a Mexican wave).

step 3:
Once all toes are off the floor, place each one carefully back down, starting with the little toe. Keep them as widely spaced as possible. Do this five times with your right foot. Then repeat five times with your left foot.

••• ✿ •••

• • • SOME USEFUL MANTRAS • • •

Mantras are sacred sounds, which are sometimes repeated during meditation to increase focus. They can be a single syllable, a single word or a series of words. Om (*see p18*) and the seed, or *bija*, mantras for the chakras (*see p24*) are among the best-known. Here are some other useful ones to learn:

MANTRA	ORIGIN	MEANING
Om mane padme hum	Buddhist mantra honouring Avalokiteshvara, the *bodhisattva* of compassion.	"Hail to the jewel in the lotus"
So hum	Yogic mantra, said to be the sound of the inhalation (*so*) and exhalation (*hum*).	"I am He (the divine)"
Om namah shivaya	Hindu mantra, honouring the higher consciousness or the inner self (represented by Shiva). The five syllables of *namah shivaya* are also thought to represent the five elements: earth, air, water, wind and fire.	"I bow to Shiva"
Gayatri mantra: **Tat savitur varenyam, bhargo devasya dhimahi, dhiyo yo nah prachodyat**	Hindu mantra from the Rig Veda (*see p43*), traditionally chanted with morning prayers.	"May we contemplate the celestial splendour of God Savitri, so that he may inspire our prayers"

• • • *PROTESTANT WHO'S WHO* • • •

Protestantism began with the Reformation of the Church in 16th-century Europe. In common usage the term is used to denote any Christian faith that is neither Roman Catholicism nor the Eastern Orthodox Church.

Adventists
Believers in the Second Coming, predicted by William Miller, a Baptist preacher, in the 1830s. Many abandoned the faith after October 2 1844, the "Great Disappointment", when Jesus did not come to Earth.

Anabaptists
Started in Zurich, Austria. Persecuted in the 16th century, for belief in adult baptism.

Baptists
Grew out of Anabaptist movement. Practised adult baptism. General Baptists see Christ's atonement as for all humankind; Particular Baptists see it as exclusive to the elect (predestined to be saved).

Calvinists
Emphasize the absolute power of God, and predestination. The name comes from John Calvin (1509–1564), a major figure in Reformed Protestantism, based in Geneva.

Congregationalists
Originated in England in the late 16th century. Each congregation governs its own affairs.

Episcopalians
Episocopal Church of the USA founded 1789 as successor to the Church of England in the American colonies.

Lutherans
Named after Martin Luther (1483–1546), whose attack on Church abuses in Germany (1417) was the catalyst for Protestantism.

Methodists/Wesleyans
Originated with John Wesley (1703–1791), who attempted to make reforms within the Church of England. Split from that Church after Wesley's death. Focus on Bible studies, simplicity of worship, "holiness of heart and life", social justice.

Pentecostalists
Emphasize personal experience of God through "baptism with the Holy Spirit". Healing and speaking in tongues play a part.

Plymouth Brethren
First congregation established in Devon, England, in 1831. Emphasis on biblical prophecy and the Second Coming.

Presbyterians
A collegiate form of Church government by pastors and elders (presbyters). The movement has roots in the Scottish Reformation.

Religious Society of Friends (Quakers)
Founded by George Fox (1624–1691). Left wing of the English Puritan movement in the 17th century. Espouses austerity, egalitarianism, pacifism.
(*See p54.*)

Reformed Churches
Term used of numerous Protestant denominations with Calvinist origins.

Restoration movement
Began in early 19th-century USA. Ambitiously sought to restore the New Testament Church established by Christ.

Seventh-day Adventists
Emphasize seeing God clearly and finding his love; the importance of scripture; and the transforming power of Jesus.

••• ✿ •••

••• A BRIEF GUIDE TO •••
MEDICAL ASTROLOGY

Each zodiac sign in Western astrology governs specific parts of the body. Being born under a particular sign is thought to predispose you to weaknesses in those areas. It can be useful to know about these:

SIGN	DATES	ASSOCIATED PARTS OF THE BODY	POTENTIAL HEALTH PROBLEMS
Aries	March 21–April 20	Head, brain, face, eyes	Headaches, fever, eye strain
Taurus	April 21–May 21	Neck, throat, thyroid gland, vocal tract	Sore throats and voice issues
Gemini	May 22–June 21	Arms, shoulders, hands, lungs, nervous system	Pneumonia, pleurisy, asthma, nerve diseases
Cancer	June 22–July 22	Stomach, breasts, chest, alimentary canal	Digestive problems, cysts, mastitis
Leo	July 23–August 22	Heart, spine, upper back	Heart problems, poor circulation
Virgo	August 23–September 22	Digestive system, intestines, spleen, pancreas, gall bladder	Digestive problems, poor absorption
Libra	September 23–October 23	Kidneys, lower back, adrenal glands, buttocks, skin	Back pain, kidney complaints
Scorpio	October 24–November 22	Genitals, reproductive and urinary systems, bowels	Infertility, urinary and bowel problems
Sagittarius	November 23–December 22	Liver, hips, thighs, sciatic nerve	Rheumatism, gout, sciatica
Capricorn	December 23–January 20	Knees, bones, joints, teeth	Weak knees, painful joints, skin complaints
Aquarius	January 21–February 19	Ankles, calves, circulation	Sprained ankles, varicose veins, blood poisoning, poor circulation
Pisces	February 20–March 20	Feet, lymphatic system, adipose tissue	Flat feet, flu, colds, excess mucus, cellulite

• • • HOMEOPATHY AT HOME • • •

Homeopathic remedies can have profound results for a wide variety of health complaints, both physiological and psychological. Unlike orthodox medicine, which prescribes illness-specific remedies, homeopathy prescribes treatments based on how illnesses manifest in each individual (*see also p76*). For chronic conditions, it's therefore essential to visit a qualified practitioner, who will take a detailed case history. For minor ailments, however, there is a range of remedies that are safe and effective for home prescription:

Aconitum napellus (Aconite): For colds, flu, high temperature with great thirst and any sudden, violent illness (take at first signs).

Apis mellifica (Apis mel.): For bites and stings.

Argentum nitricum (Arg. nit.): For fear of flying (with anxiety and upset stomach) and fear of failure (take before important events); also for overwork, mental strain and headaches.

Arnica montana (Arnica): For relief from shocks; also before and after surgery to reduce swelling and bruising.

Arsenicum album (Arsen. alb.): For food poisoning and gastric upsets with burning pains.

Belladonna (Belladonna): For fever, sore throats, headaches and earaches.

Bryonia alba (Bryonia): For dry coughs and chesty colds.

Gelsemium sempervirens (Gelsemium): For flu, especially if symptoms include aching limbs, sore throat, runny nose, shivering, sneezing or difficulty swallowing.

Ignatia amara (Ignatia): For emotional shock, such as grief (with aconite if the emotion is unexpected); also for fainting and hysteria.

Nux vomica (Nux vom.): For indigestion, constipation and travel sickness; also good after food or alcohol over-indulgence.

• CHUANG TZU'S BUTTERFLY •

Chuang Tzu was a Taoist sage in the 4th century BCE. One night he dreamed that he was a butterfly, happily flitting here and there. When he woke up, he puzzled about the dream. Was he a man who had dreamed he was a butterfly? Or was he a butterfly now dreaming it was a man?

Chuang Tzu's dream poses philosophical questions: How do we know when we're awake and when we're dreaming? How do we know if what we perceive is real or illusion? Are we sleeping souls (trapped in our bodies, like a caterpillar in its chrysalis) or awakened beings (as free as any butterfly)? Perhaps it's only in recognizing the impermanence of all wordly distinctions that we can set ourselves free, on the path to true "awakening". We can never truly know *what* we are – only *that* we are.

Ra (or Re)

Sun god. The supreme deity, ancestor of the pharaohs. Prime source of cosmic energy. Regulated time and the seasons. His daily re-emergence from Duat, the Underworld, symbolizes the cyclical nature of creation.

Thoth

Divine scribe. Ra's mouthpiece. Depicted with the head of an ibis. Associated with magic, writing and science. Calculated the movements of the heavenly bodies.

Anubis

God of embalming. Depicted with the head of a jackal. Presided over mummification and the passage to the Underworld.

Osiris

God of the Underworld. Associated with death, rebirth and fertility. The judge encountered by the souls of the dead in the Hall of Two Truths. Also linked with the sprouting of vegetation at the annual Nile flooding.

Isis

Wife (and sister) of Osiris. When her husband was killed and dismembered by jealous Seth, who scattered the body parts far and wide, she tracked them down and used magic to revive him for long enough to conceive a son, Horus. The annual Nile flooding was said to be caused by the tears she shed for her dead husband.

Horus

Sky god. Depicted with the head of a falcon. Son of Osiris and Isis. Embodied the idea of divine kingship, with the pharaohs as his representatives on Earth. His left eye represented the moon; his right, the sun. Eventually avenged his father's murder by vanquishing Seth.

Seshat

Goddess of wisdom, knowledge and writing. Depicted with a papyrus stem protruding from her head. Divine scribe and surveyor. Also associated with architecture, astronomy and building.

Ma'at

Goddess of justice, order, truth. Ostrich feather headdress. Responsible for the cycle of birth and death, growth and harvesting of crops, annual Nile flooding. The hearts of the deceased were weighed against her feather of truth – for Osiris to establish which souls could pass into the afterlife.

• • • *ABRACADABRA* • • •

Although most widely known nowadays as a magician's conjuring spell, the word "Abracadabra" has a long history as a healing incantation. In a 2nd-century poem entitled *De Medicina Praecepta*, Serenus Sammonicus, physician to the Roman Emperor Flavius Valerius Severus, recommended wearing the word "Abracadabra" on a charm around the neck to cure fevers and asthma. The letters were to be arranged in an inverted triangle (see below): as they disappeared toward the bottom of the triangle, so supposedly did any illness or bad luck. Such an amulet was to be worn for nine days, before being tossed into a stream.

```
A - B - R - A - C - A - D - A - B - R - A
A - B - R - A - C - A - D - A - B - R
A - B - R - A - C - A - D - A - B
A - B - R - A - C - A - D - A
A - B - R - A - C - A - D
A - B - R - A - C - A
A - B - R - A - C
A - B - R - A
A - B - R
A - B
A
```

••• ❀ •••

• • • *CRYSTAL CHAKRA HEALING* • • •

Crystal therapists often arrange crystals in special healing patterns on the body to restore balance and enhance well-being. One technique involves placing crystals on or near each of the seven main *chakra* points (*see p24*) while the subject is supine. Below are the crystals most commonly used for each chakra, with a note on where they are usually placed:

Root chakra *(on the floor at the base of the spine or around the feet):* hematite, smoky quartz, black tourmaline, tiger's eye

Sacral chakra *(just above the pelvic bone):* bloodstone, garnet, jasper, ruby

Solar plexus chakra *(in or on the navel):* citrine, malachite, pyrite, rhodochrosite

Heart chakra *(on the heart area):* aventurine, emerald, green calcite, lepidolite, rose quartz, tourmaline

Throat chakra *(on the throat):* aquamarine, celestite, larimar, lapis lazuli, sapphire, sodalite, turquoise

Brow chakra *(between the eyebrows):* amethyst, azurite, sodalite, moss agate, sugilite

Crown chakra *(on the floor above the head):* diamond, snowy quartz, white jade, white tourmaline, danburite

• THE THREE RANKS OF DRUIDISM •

Many modern druids recognize three classes, or ranks, of membership – believed, with much conjecture, to follow the ancient Celtic orders.

Bard: Mainly responsible for poetry, music, storytelling. Trained for at least nine years, learning around 20,0000 verses.

Ovate *(or vate):* Mainly responsible for prophecy, astrology and sacrificial ritual.

Druid: Mainly responsible for teaching, administration and law. Druids also acted as priests, performing sacred ceremonies.

••• ❀ •••

• • • MAJOR JEWISH FESTIVALS • • •

Purim *(Festival of Lots):* A one-day festival four weeks before Pesach. Commemorates the story of Esther.

Pesach *(Passover):* An eight-day festival in Nisan (March/April). Celebrates the freedom of the Israelites from enslavement in Egypt. No leavened food is allowed. On the first two nights the Seder (service and celebration that tell of the Passover and Exodus) is held at home.

Shavuot *(Pentecost):* A two-day festival seven weeks after Pesach. Honours Moses being given the Ten Commandments.

Rosh Hashanah *(New Year):* First of the Ten Days of Repentance. Held in Tishri (September/October). A time for celebration but also for reflection on sins committed in the previous year.

Yom Kippur *(Day of Atonement):* Last of the Ten Days of Repentance. The most solemn High Holy Day in Judaism, when people pray for forgiveness for their sins.

Succot *(Feast of Tabernacles, or Feast of Booths):* Starts five days after Yom Kippur. Commemorates the 40 years the Israelites spent in the wilderness and the temporary dwellings or "booths" *(succah)* they built and lived in during this time – with walls of wood and ceilings of greenery. The eighth day is the *Shemini Atzeret* (the Eighth Day of Solemn Assembly). At the end of Succot is *Simchat Torah* (Rejoicing of the Law) – a festival celebrating the completion of the annual cycle of weekly Torah readings in the synagogue.

Chanukah *(Festival of Lights):* An eight-day festival in Kislev (November/December). Marks the victory of the Maccabees over their Hellenistic oppressors, and the re-dedication of the Temple of Jerusalem. The Maccabees found enough oil to light the temple's "eternal flame" for only one day, yet it miraculously stayed alight for eight days.

✦ ✳ ✦

DIY HAND REFLEXOLOGY:
SOLVING COMMON AILMENTS

Professional reflexologists usually work on the feet (*see p50*). However, the hands also have numerous reflex points – mainly on the palm side. Easy to reach for DIY purposes, these can be worked safely and effectively for a range of problems. Work firmly, with the pad of your thumb, as follows:

To ease eye strain: Make small circling movements (clockwise) over the top crease of your index finger; first on your right hand, then left.

To relieve headache: Apply pressure to the end of your thumb – hold for 5 seconds and release; first on the right hand, then the left. Repeat.

To combat indigestion, nausea or constipation: Apply pressure across the centre of your palm, from your little finger toward your thumb; first on the right hand, then the left.

To alleviate neck and shoulder tension: Rub around the bases of your index and middle fingers; first on the right hand, then the left.

To lessen sinus problems: Massage down your thumb, from tip to base, then repeat on each finger; first on the right hand, then the left.

To soothe a sore throat: Apply pressure around the base of your thumb; first on the right hand, then the left.

••• ✸ •••

• THE THREE SYMBOLS OF REIKI •

Students of Reiki (*see p65*) are taught three special symbols to visualize when giving treatments. However, these symbols are believed to have power only once practitioners have been initiated into the second degree of Reiki (between first degree and Reiki master).

Cho Ku Rei (Power Symbol): focuses energy before a Reiki session.	***Ki*** (Symbol of Emotional and Mental Strength): helps to eliminate harmful patterns and bring about positive changes.	***Hon Sha Ze Sho Nen*** (Distant Healing Symbol): used to perform healing sessions from afar.

• • • JAIN COSMOLOGY • • •

According to Jain doctrine, which has no place for a creator, the universe, or *loka*, exists eternally and consists of three realms: Upper World, Middle World, Nether World. Some scholars present this as a five-tier system, by treating sub-realms of the Upper and Nether Worlds (Supreme Abode and Base) as realms in their own right. This account proceeds downward:

1. **The Supreme Abode** *(Siddhsilla):* At the top of the universe. Shaped like an inverted umbrella. The resting place of all liberated souls (*siddha*).

2. **The Upper World** *(Urdhavlok):* Above the peak of Mount Meru (holy mountain of the Middle World). Spindle-shaped. Has many levels, inhabited by various classes of celestial beings and gods.

3. **The Middle World** *(Madhyalok):* Made up of large continents surrounded by oceans.

Mount Meru (on which the Upper World sits) is in the middle of the central continent, Jambudvipa. Includes the Earth, so is the realm of humans, animals and plants.

4. **The Nether World** *(Adholok):* Includes seven levels of hell, each inhabited by a different type of demon. The lowest is for those who have committed the worst sins.

5. **The Base** *(Nigoda):* Beneath the seventh hell, inhabited by the lowest forms of life. Also called "the storehouse of bonded souls".

•••✿•••

• • • YOGIC SLEEP • • •

Yoga nidra, or "yogic sleep" is a restful practice, particularly useful at the end of the day as it encourages withdrawal from the outside world, and movement down through levels of consciousness to a state of inner peace. This is an advanced technique and, after trying the taster exercise below, you may find the guidance of a yoga teacher helpful in mastering it.

1. Lie down in a quiet space. Close your eyes and breathe slowly and deeply.

2. Take your awareness to your right foot – contract the muscles there, then completely relax them. Next, take your awareness up to your knee and do the same there. Then to your right hip, the right side of your stomach, ribs and chest and your right shoulder. Continue the process down your right arm to your hand, then back up to your neck, jaw, face and scalp – letting go of any tension you find along the way.

3. Do the same in reverse order down the left side of your body, from arm and shoulder to foot.

4. Now bring your awareness to your breath. Notice the rise and fall of your chest and abdomen, and the sensation of the air entering and leaving your nostrils. Rest here for between 20 and 45 minutes, but try not to become so relaxed that you fall asleep.

• • • PLANET SYMBOLS • • •

Below are symbols astrologers use to denote the "planets" (including the sun and moon) as well as their various associations. Where a metal is given, these planet symbols were also used by alchemists, to refer to the metal linked with them. The bracketed planet names are alternative terms used by alchemists.

PLANET	SYMBOL	METAL	ATTRIBUTES	GREEK DEITY
Earth	⊕ * (see below)	—	—	Gaia
Sun (Sol)	☉	Gold	Action Vitality Energy	Helios
Moon (Luna)	☽	Silver	Emotion Mystery Intuition	Selene, Artemis
Mercury (Mercurius)	☿	Sulphur, Mercury	Intellect Understanding Communication	Hermes
Venus	♀	Copper	Beauty Harmony Attraction	Aphrodite
Mars	♂	Iron	Energy Strength Initiative	Aries
Jupiter	♃	Tin	Belief Travel Expansion	Zeus
Saturn	♄	Lead	Control Wisdom Fixation	Cronus
Uranus	⛢ ⛢ (both used)	—	Transformation Invention Revolution	Uranos
Neptune	♆	—	Idealism Blending Collective unconscious	Poseidon
Pluto	♇	—	Rebirth Renewal Occult power	Hades

* In astrology, the circle symbolizes spirit and the cross physical matter – a circle with a cross in it therefore symbolizes the Earth. In prehistoric times, however, the same symbol was used to represent the sun (*see p14*) – most likely for the simple reason that the circle resembled the shape of the sun in the sky and the arms of the cross resembled its rays.

• • • *RELAXING VISUALIZATION* • • •

A positive visualization can be an effective way to release stress, as it encourages the mind and the body to work in harmony to unwind. Spend as little or as long as you feel you need on the following exercise:

1. Lie down and make yourself comfortable. Become aware of your breathing but don't attempt to change it. Close your eyes.

2. Tune into the grounded sensation of your body on the floor. Allow any tension to drain off you, into the ground beneath. Enjoy the feeling of being entirely supported.

3. Imagine you're lying under a beautiful, golden sun. Feel the gentle warmth of the sun's rays sinking softly into your body, through every pore in your skin. Relax into this state of receptivity.

4. Visualize the warmth running gently through your body like shining, liquid gold, cleansing you of stress and heaviness, filling you instead with ease and contentment. If there are areas of your body that feel particularly tight or tense, direct more of the sun's healing energy here to melt any blockages. Take your time doing this, savouring each moment.

5. When you feel ready, bring your attention back to your breath for a few minutes, breathing deeply and evenly.

6. Start to notice the sounds around you. Wiggle your fingers and toes, and come back to normal waking awareness. Roll over onto one side and slowly bring yourself to a sitting or standing position.

• *THE SEVEN SORROWS OF MARY* •

Seven distressing events in the life of the Virgin Mary are accorded particular significance in the Catholic Church. These "sorrows" provide a focus for devotional meditation on Mary's suffering and sacrifice:

1. Simeon's prophecy, on seeing the infant Jesus, that a sword would pierce Mary's heart (alluding to his later crucifixion).

2. Flight of Mary, Joseph and Jesus to Egypt – to escape King Herod's Massacre of the Innocents.

3. Mary and Joseph losing Jesus (aged 12) for three days, before finding him in the Temple.

4. Mary's meeting with Jesus as he carried the cross to Golgotha.

5. Jesus's crucifixion, with Mary at the foot of the cross.

6. The body of Jesus being taken down from the cross and placed in Mary's arms.

7. The burial of Jesus at the tomb of Joseph of Arimathea.

• COLOUR SYMBOLISM •

Colours have powerful symbolic resonances. Here are some of the most common associations with ten colours across a range of cultures:

Black: Darkness, sickness, death, evil, mourning (except in the East). Time/Kali (Hindu). Rebirth (Egyptian).

White: Light, holiness, perfection, innocence, surrender. Mourning (Chinese). Enlightenment (Tibetan).

Red: Fire, passion, energy, rage, war. Ares/Mars (Greek/Roman). Good luck (Chinese).

Yellow: Faithlessness, cowardice, betrayal. Joy and optimism. Humility (Buddhist). Courage (Japanese). Mourning (Egyptian).

Green: Life, death and rebirth. Hope and immortality. Satan (Christian). Death (Celtic). Spring (Greek/Roman).

Blue: Vastness, infinity, coldness, the ultimate, fate. Virgin Mary, Queen of Heaven (Christian).

Violet: Devotion, passion balanced by reason, grief. Passion of Christ (Christian).

Purple: Royalty, majesty, power, spirituality. Zeus/Jupiter (Greek/Roman).

Brown: Earth, fertility, poverty. Humility (Catholic).

Gold: Divine power, intuition, illumination, intellect, the sun (all corn and sun deities).

• • • *THE JAPANESE EMPERORS'* • • •
LEGENDARY ANCESTRY

Two books that created a mythic prelude to history, commissioned by Empress Gemmei in the 8th century CE and known as the *Kojiki* and the *Nohingi*, reinforced the central role of Japan's ruling dynasty by tracing its ancestry from the time of creation through to the birth of the first emperor, Jimmu. Below is a summary of this unbroken lineage:

1. **Inzanagi and Izanami:** Among the first generation of gods, hatched from the cosmic egg. These divine siblings populated the Earth with many gods and spirits, the greatest of them being the sun goddess Amaterasu and the moon god Tsukiyomi.

2. **Amaterasu and Tsukiyomi:** Lived as man and wife, but fell out with one another when Tsukiyomi killed the food goddess Ogetsuno. Then avoided each other, as the sun and moon have done ever since.

3. **Honinigi:** Amaterasu's grandson, sent to Earth to rule as her representative. Married the earthly princess Konohana. Had two sons, Honosusori and Hikohoho (known in English as Fireshine and Fireshade).

4. *Hikohobo:* The younger of Honinigi's two sons, he travelled to an underwater kingdom, where he fell in love with the princess Toyotama (daughter of Ryujin, the Japanese sea god). She returned to land with him for just long enough to bear him a child, Ugaya. Toyotama's sister Tamayori stayed to help to raise the boy.

5. *Ugaya:* Eventually married his aunt, Tamayori. Together they had five children, one of whom was Iwarebiko.

▼

6. *Iwarebiko (known as Jimmu):* Became the first emperor of Japan, c.660BCE, according to traditional lists. The same dynasty has ruled ever since. (As recently as 1945, the Japanese emperor officially claimed a direct line of descent to the sun goddess Amaterasu.)

• • • THE 99 NAMES OF ALLAH • • •

On the basis of the Qur'an and the *hadith* (the corpus of sayings attributed to the Prophet Mohammed), medieval Islamic scholars compiled a list of 99 divine attributes, more commonly known as the 99 Names of God. Today, Muslim children are encouraged to memorize a list of these names, which are sometimes recited in song:

The Compassionate, The Caring, The Sovereign, The Holy, The Source of Peace, The Faith-giver, The Protector, The Almighty, The Compeller, The Greatest, The Creator, The Rightful, The Shaper, The Forgiver, The Subduer, The Giver, The Provider, The Opener, The Omniscient, The Restrainer, The Expander, The Abaser, The Exalter, The Giver of Honour, The Humiliator, The Hearer, The Seer, The Judge, The Just, The Subtle, The All-aware, The Forebearing, The Magnificent, The Merciful, The Grateful, The Exalted, The Sublime, The Preserver, The Nourisher, The Accounter, The Majestic, The Generous, The Overseer, The Responder, The Vast, The Wise, The Loving, The Glorious, The Resurrector, The Witness, The Truth (or The Real), The Entrusted, The Strong, The Firm, The Guardian, The Praiseworthy, The Appraiser, The Initiator, The Restorer, The Life-giver, The Life-taker, The Ever-living, The Sustainer, The Finder, The Illustrious, The One, The Indivisible, The Everlasting, The Able, The Determiner, The Expediter, The Delayer, The First, The Last, The Apparent, The Hidden, The Patron, The Supreme, The Righteous, The Guide to Repentance, The Avenger, The Pardoner, The Clement, The Owner of All, The Lord of Majesty and Bounty, The Equitable, The Gatherer, The Wealthy, The Enricher, The Preventer, The Afflictor, The Benefactor, The Light, The Guide, The Originator, The One Who Remains, The Inheritor, The Great Teacher, The Patient One

+►─✳─◄+

• *THE WAY TO EGYPTIAN PARADISE* •

The *Book of the Dead*, or *Book of Coming Forth by Day*, was the most common of the texts left in the burial chambers of ancient Egyptians (*see p52*). It chronicled the journey of the deceased through the Underworld to the court of Osiris, where it would be judged whether he or she was worthy of eternal life in paradise (the "Field of Reeds"). A selection of spells was included, to help the deceased overcome obstacles on the way. Some of these are shown below:

Amulet spell: to infuse with power an amulet placed on the deceased's neck.

Opening the Mouth spell: to enable the deceased to speak in the afterlife.

Seven Arits spell: to allow the deceased to pass through the seven guarded halls or *arits*.

Ferry Boat spell: to summon a boat to the banks of the river in the underworld.

Divine Judges spell: to help protest the deceased's innocence in front of 42 judges.

Weighing of the Heart spell: to prevent the deceased's heart from weighing down the scales when weighed against Ma'at's "feather of truth" (*see p52*).

Shabti spell: to empower *shabti* (funerary statuettes) to perform agricultural labour in the Field of Reeds on behalf of the deceased.

Transformation spell: to turn the deceased into a god.

••• ✿ •••

• • • *HOW TO LOCATE LEY LINES* • • •

Ley lines are straight alignments of three or more ancient sites, sometimes described as circuits of Earth energy, with the power to alter human consciousness (like a global equivalent of meridians: *see p68*). Alfred Watkins popularized them in his book *The Old Straight Track* (1925), which traced many in Britain. Here is a guide to finding them yourself:

1. Scan a large-scale map (old maps tend to be most productive) of your chosen area for: ancient monuments, stone circles, megaliths, mounds, barrows, cairns, tumuli, wells, moats, beacon points, cathedrals, churches, hermitages, castles, burial sites.

2. Circle any such features. Then place the end of a ruler at one of these points, and swing the ruler around to see if two or more of the other ringed points align with it. If not, repeat the process, each time starting from a different ringed feature. If you find a convincing alignment, draw it on the map and check for further points along the same line.

3. Walk your suspected ley: you might find sites unmarked on maps. Ask local residents if they know of legends attached to landscape features. Check out old place names, which may hint at further ancient sites.

··· SEVEN FAMOUS ···
HINDU TEMPLES

For Hindus, the temple is the place where gods and people meet – the cosmic pillar that links Heaven and Earth. It's also symbolic of Mount Meru, the many-layered cosmic mountain at the centre of the universe. Each Hindu temple houses an image of its presiding deity. The earliest surviving temples were carved out of rock. The great age of temple building was c.500–1500 – at the same time as many of the great cathedrals of Europe were being built.

Brihadisvara Temple,
Thanjavur, Tamil Nadu:
11th-century temple, primarily dedicated to Shiva. The *vimana,* or temple tower, is 215ft (66m) high. A 16ft (6.2m) long figure of Shiva's mount, the bull Nandi (*see p102*), is carved from a single block of granite.

Kandariya Mahadeva Temple,
Khajuraho, Madhya Pradesh:
Largest and most elaborate of the 24 temples built from the 9th to the 12th centuries at this major site. Dedicated to Shiva (Mahadeva). Famous for erotic sculptures on the walls, thought to celebrate the marriage of Shiva and Parvati – or possibly to serve as a love manual.

Konark Sun Temple, *Orissa:*
13th-century temple dedicated to the sun god, Surya. Conceived as a gigantic chariot, with twelve pairs of wheels, to carry the sun god on his daily journey across the sky. Famous for its human and animal sculptures, including many erotic couples.

Prambanan, *Java:* Near
Borobodur. Built c.850ce. One of the largest Hindu temple complexes in SE Asia, with shrines to many deities. Reconstructed between 1918 and 1953, having fallen into disrepair.

Sun Temple, *Modhera, Gujarat:*
11th-century temple dedicated to the sun god, Surya. Its east–west layout is so precisely calibrated that the sun's rays strike the centre of the inner sanctum at noon precisely at each equinox. Also famous for its *kund:* a large, stepped rectangular "pond", with 108 (an auspicious number in Hinduism: *see p128*) miniature shrines carved between its steps.

Ekambareswarar,
Kanchipuram, Tamil Nadu:
Started in the 1st century. One of five major Shiva temples that represent the five elements – this one symbolizes earth. Renowned for its thousand-pillared hall, or *mandapam,* and 1,008 *lingams* (pillar-like icons). Boasts one of the tallest temple towers in South India. Site of a sacred mango tree, 3,500 years old.

Minakshi Temple, *Madurai,*
Tamil Nadu: 17th-century temple built on an ancient site. Symbolically important to the Tamil people. Dedicated to Shiva (Sundareshvara) and Parvati (Minakshi). Features twelve huge, ornately sculpted and painted towers, or *gopuras:* the tallest rises to more than 160ft (50m). Reconsecrated every twelve years, at which time all sculptures are repaired, repainted or replaced.

• • • BRAVE AS A WARRIOR • • •

According to Hindu legend, Daksha, father of the god Shiva's first consort, Sati, strongly opposed their union. To humiliate his son-in-law, he organized an important sacrifice and invited every god except for Shiva. Sati's dishonour was so great that she immolated herself. Then Shiva, infuriated, plucked a lock of hair from his head and cast it on the ground. From it arose Virabhadra – a terrifying, dark-skinned warrior, with burning eyes and a thousand arms. Shiva sent his creation to destroy Daksha and his armies, which he did decisively.

The three empowering yoga *asanas* known as the Warrior Poses – *Virabhadrasana I, II and III* – are named after this mythic warrior incarnation of Shiva. Practise one or all of these postures any time you need an injection of warrior-like strength.

Virabhadrasana I
1. Stand with your feet about 3ft (1m) apart and parallel.
2. Turn your right foot out 90 degrees and your left foot in 45 degrees. Turn your hips to face your right foot.
3. Exhale and bend your right knee, aiming to create a right-angle between your upper and lower legs.
4. Inhale and reach your arms upward, palms facing each other. Look up between your hands.
5. Inhale and come back up to centre.
Repeat the exercise on the other side.

Virabhadrasana II
1. Stand with your feet about 3ft (1m) apart and parallel.
2. Turn your right foot out 90 degrees and your left foot in slightly. Keep your hips facing forward.
3. Exhale and bend your right knee, aiming to create a right-angle between your upper and lower legs. Roll your left hip back to make sure your hips don't twist to the right.
4. Inhale and lift your arms out to the sides at shoulder height, keeping your shoulders relaxed. Turn your head to look along your right arm.
5. Inhale and come back to centre.
Repeat the exercise on the other side.

Virabhadrasana III
1. Stand in Virabhadrasana I, with your right leg bent, your arms above your head and your hips and upper body facing right.
2. Step your left foot about 6in (15cm) toward your right, without changing the position of your hips.

3. Exhale and bend your torso down toward your right thigh, bringing your arms out in front of you, parallel with the floor.

4. Inhale and straighten your front leg and lift your back leg behind you, letting your torso move further forward to come into a balance. Stay here for a moment, looking forward and flexing the foot if comfortable.

5. Exhale and bring your left foot to the floor. Inhale, bring your torso to vertical and step your feet together. Repeat the exercise on the other side.

••• ✿ •••

• • • *HOLY SITES OF ISLAM* • • •

The Sacred Mosque (Masjid al-Haram), Mecca, Saudi Arabia
Holiest site in Islam and largest mosque in the world, holding up to 800,000 worshippers during the annual *hajj* pilgrimage. Built around the Kaaba, a cube-shaped structure toward which Muslims worldwide direct their daily prayers. Embedded in the Kaaba's wall is the Black Stone, believed to be a meteorite placed there by the patriarch Abraham.

Mosque of the Prophet (Masjid al-Nabawi), Medina, S. Arabia
Second holiest site in Islam. Built on the site of the house where the Prophet Mohammed lived after making the *hijra* (migration) to Medina – the event from which the first year of the Islamic calendar is dated. The central feature is the green dome that covers Mohammed's tomb.

The Al-Aqsa Mosque, Jerusalem, Israel
Contains the Dome of the Rock, built at the spot from which Mohammed is said to have made his famed "night journey" to heaven. The mosque, constructed up to 705CE, stands on the Temple Mount, where King Solomon supposedly built his temple.

Tomb of Imam Ali, Najaf, Iraq
Holiest site of Shi'ism; only Mecca and Medina receive more annual pilgrims. Shi'ite Muslims believe Ali, cousin and son-in-law of Mohammed, to be Mohammed's legitimate successor.

Tomb of Imam Husayn, Karbala, Iraq
Houses the remains of Imam Husayn ibn Ali, second grandson of Mohammed, who according to Shi'ites was martyred as he tried to stake his claim to the caliphate – the leadership of Islam (*see p17*).

Grand Mosque of Damascus (Umayyad Mosque), Syria
One of the largest and oldest mosques. Features shrines that contain the heads of John the Baptist and of the Shi'ite martyr Husayn ibn Ali.

Harar, Ethiopia
A city with special significance for African Muslims, with 82 mosques and 102 shrines. A major commercial centre, it was linked with the Arabian Peninsula via trade routes in Mohammed's day.

• • • STORECUPBOARD HEALING • • •

All ancient systems of healthcare teach that well-being starts with healthy, balanced eating. In addition, many nutritious foodstuffs have hidden healing powers and can be used in unexpected ways:

Beetroot: Include in fresh juices to help to flush the kidneys. (Avoid if diabetic.)

Cabbage: Iron a large leaf and apply as a hot poultice on swollen or inflamed areas.

Cucumber: Slice and lay on sore eyes or sunburned skin for a cooling effect.

Egg whites: Dab onto a baby's skin in three layers to soothe nappy rash (let each layer dry before applying the next).

Garlic: Eat raw cloves to fight infections, colds or viruses. Apply crushed cloves to treat athlete's foot or thrush. Place 4 drops of garlic oil on cotton wool and place in ear to ease earache.

Honey: Apply directly to wounds or dilute with hot water and lemon for colds, coughs or sore throats. Taken for insomnia in Japan. Local honey is said to help to prevent hayfever.

Lemon: Dab on spots and bites to ease the sting. With hot water and honey makes a soothing drink for colds, flus or catarrh.

Mustard: Make a paste with a tablespoon of mustard and a little water, then dissolve in a bath to combat colds or flu.

Olive oil: Add 7 drops of rosemary essential oil per tablespoon of warm olive oil, and massage into the hips to ease sciatica pain. (Avoid if epileptic.)

Onions: Chop an onion, cover with runny honey and leave overnight, then sip 1 tablespoon of the onion-infused liquid every 2 hours to ease coughs.

Salt: Gargle with a salt solution (1 teaspoon of sea salt to half a cup of warm water) up to six times a day to ease a sore throat.

Sultanas/raisins: Eat regularly to avoid constipation.

• HOW TO MAKE A SMUDGE STICK •

Widely used in shamanic practices, smudge sticks are bundles of sacred herbs that people light to waft the smoke around any place or person they wish to "cleanse" of negative energy. Making your own smudge stick is said to deepen your connection with the spirits of the herbs, giving greater power to any rituals or ceremonies you perform with it.

1. Ideally, pick fresh herbs* as they bloom during a waxing moon; otherwise buy them. Approach each plant with respect, take what you need – a few pieces 8–12in (20–30cm) long – and leave a pinch of cornmeal or tobacco at the root of each plant afterwards with your thanks.
*Caution: Don't use dried herbs as they flare too easily.

2. Take quite a thick stick of plant as a base, arrange the other stems around it, and firmly wind a piece of cotton around the bundle to hold everything together – start at the bottom and end about halfway up.

3. Hang the smudge stick, by the tied end, somewhere warm and dry until the plants are almost dry, but not totally moisture-free.

Possible Plants to Use
* *Sagebrush* (not culinary sage): transforms energy and brings change
* *Sweetgrass:* attracts positive energy
* *Lavender:* restores balance and attracts loving energy
* *Cedar:* clears negative emotions
* *Juniper:* purifies and creates sacred space
* *Yerba Santa:* purifies, and sets and protects boundaries
* *Rosemary:* brings clarity to problems

••• ✿ •••

THE EIGHTFOLD EXAMINATION OF AYURVEDA

The *astavidha pariksha* (eightfold examination) of ayurvedic medicine involves detailed observation of the body to assess which *dosha* (see p115) is out of balance, so that curative measures can be taken.

1. **Pulse** *(nadi pariksha):* Taken on the wrist – if *vata* is aggravated, the pulse may be irregular; if *pitta*, it "jumps like a frog"; if *kapha*, it's "slow like a swan".

2. **Tongue** *(jihva pariksha):* If *vata* is aggravated, the tongue is dry, rough and cracked; if *pitta*, it's red and hot; if *kapha*, it's slimy and coated.

3. **Voice** *(sabda pariksha):* If *vata* is aggravated, the voice may be hoarse; if *pitta*, it may seem cracked; if *kapha*, it may appear heavy and sluggish.

4. **Skin** *(sparsa pariksha):* Both the look and temperature are assessed – if *vata* is aggravated, it causes low temperature and coarse skin; if *pitta*, high temperature; if *kapha*, cold, damp skin.

5. **Eyes** *(drka pariksha):* If *vata* is aggravated, it can cause dry, sunken eyes; if *pitta*, they may be red, yellow or burning; if *kapha*, possibly watery, with heavy eyelids.

6. **General appearance** *(akrti pariksha):* A variety of clues (from colour of face to shape of fingernails) can lead to diagnosis.

7. **Urine** *(mutra pariksha):* The quantity, colour and texture are assessed, and whether the urine is foaming or not. Traditionally, a drop of oil was added to the sample – if it spread over the surface, the disease was curable; if it sank, it was incurable.

8. **Stools** *(mala pariksha):* If *vata* is aggravated, this causes a hard, dry, pale stool; if *pitta*, green or yellow liquid; if *kapha*, white and mucus-streaked.

• • • FENG SHUI IN ACTION • • •

Famously good feng shui

HSBC Bank Headquarters, Hong Kong (1985): Architect Norman Foster contrived a direct view of the harbour (because water symbolizes financial success). Escalators are angled against the entrance to prevent evil spirits from flowing in.

Trump International Hotel, New York (1997): On the advice of feng shui experts, tycoon Donald Trump commissioned a huge steel globe to deflect the negative energies of passing traffic away from the entrance.

Burj Al Arab Hotel, Dubai (1999): Its curved, sail-like structure and proximity to the sea combine the two most important feng shui elements: wind and water.

St Paul's Cathedral, London (1697): The dome channels and harnesses the chi of heaven, promoting calm and spiritual well-being in anyone who sits below.

The White House, Washington, D.C. (1800): The front lawn provides an open, unobstructed space where chi can circulate healthily before entering the building. This is called a ming tang, or "bright hall".

Taipei 101 Tower, Taiwan (2004): Resembles a bamboo stalk – therefore symbolizes strength and vigour. Organized into eight sections of eight floors (eight is a lucky number). The swirling waters of a fountain by the entrance disperse aggressive energy from the long, straight road running up to the tower.

Famously bad feng shui

American Stock Exchange, New York (1921): The small entrance reduces the amount of chi that can enter. The building also has excessive yin (passive) energy owing to its position downhill from a cemetery.

The Millennium Dome, London (1999): Resembles a rice bowl with incense sticks poking out – traditionally placed at shrines of the deceased in China. The dome is therefore a death symbol.

Sydney Opera House (1973): The triangular shapes of the roof make this a fire element building, ideal for an arts venue. But its position next to water causes a clash of energies, which could lead to disagreements among those who use it.

Bank of China, Hong Kong (1989): Sharp corners and "X" motifs act as what are called "poison arrows", directing negative energy toward the neighbouring buildings as well as back onto itself.

Houses for the TV series "Big Brother", USA and UK (since 2000): Designers deliberately break feng shui rules, using clashing colours and juxtaposed mirrors that amplify discordant energies, to create an atmosphere of tension.

Taj Mahal, India (1648): Surprisingly, the narrow, reflective pool and the two pathways that lead up to the mausoleum direct harmful energy straight to the centre.

Longwang

Scaled, five-clawed, immortal Chinese "dragon kings" with serpentine bodies, and heads adorned with horns and whiskers. Symbolize royal power. Live in splendid underwater palaces, feeding on opals and pearls. Can stir up typhoons and whirlpools when they rise to the sea's surface and create storms when they take to the air. Their powers give them a life-or-death hold over all who live nearby.

Ryu

Wingless, serpent-like beings. Closely related to the Longwang, but with three claws instead of five. One of the four divine beasts of Japanese mythology (the others being the crimson bird, the black turtle and the white tiger) – all adaptations of

Chinese constellation symbols. More slender than other Oriental dragons, they fly less frequently. Closely connected with the sea, as Japan, unlike China, is surrounded by the ocean. Also often used as the emblem of the Emperor and the hero. The Japanese emperor Hirohito traced his ancestry back 125 generations to Princess Fruitful Jewel, daughter of a Ryu.

Celtic Dragons

Typically four-legged, winged and fire-breathing. Also come in the form of serpents (Lindworms). Represent sovereignty and power. Associated too with the land: druids believed that the Earth itself was the body of the dragon, and the perceived "path of the dragons" was thought to be critical to the energy flow, or "ley", of the landscape.

After the introduction of Christianity, dragons became associated with paganism and evil, to be defeated in tales such as that of St George. However, the Welsh red dragon (*Ddraig Gymreig*) remains the official symbol on the country's flag.

Norse Dragons

Scaled, winged and fire-breathing. Feature in Nordic tales such as *Siegfried and Fáfnir*, in which the gold-hoarding dragon Fáfnir is

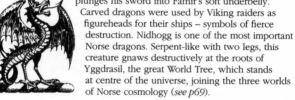

defeated by Siegfried: the latter hides in a pit and plunges his sword into Fáfnir's soft underbelly. Carved dragons were used by Viking raiders as figureheads for their ships – symbols of fierce destruction. Nidhogg is one of the most important Norse dragons. Serpent-like with two legs, this creature gnaws destructively at the roots of Yggdrasil, the great World Tree, which stands at centre of the universe, joining the three worlds of Norse cosmology (*see p69*).

• • • THE TRIALS OF ODYSSEUS • • •

Homer's *Odyssey* recounts the travails of the Greek commander Odysseus (Ulysses to the Romans) on his voyage home to the island of Ithaca from the Trojan War. Delayed by a succession of disasters, he took ten years to complete the journey. The trials that he and his men faced included:

• A battle with the inhabitants of the island of the Cicones, where they had taken temporary shelter.

• Landing on the island of the Lotus Eaters, where the sailors were drugged and lost all interest in returning home.

• Confronting the Cyclopes, one-eyed giants, on their island.

• Being captured by Polyphemus, cannibalistic son of Poseidon. They escaped by blinding him.

• Being given a bag containing the contrary winds by Aeolus (a mortal who had been granted control over these forces). Despite strict instructions not to open the bag, two of the crew took a peek just before reaching Ithaca, releasing a storm that drove the ship back to Aeolia.

• Visiting the land of the Laestrygonians, cannibal giants who destroyed all but one of the ships and ate many of the crew.

• Falling under the spell of Circe, an enchantress who transformed some of the men into pigs. She turned them back into humans only when Odysseus agreed to stay with her for a year.

• Journeying to the Underworld to consult the shade of Tiresias, a blind prophet who could foretell the future, including the hero's voyage home.

• Avoiding the lure of the Sirens, who tempted sailors to their death with beautiful song. On Circe's advice, Odysseus filled the crew's ears with beeswax and had himself lashed to the mast.

• Sailing through a narrow strait bordered on one side by the six-headed monster Scylla, and on the other by Charybdis, a nymph transformed into a deadly whirlpool. Steering too close to Scylla, Odysseus lost six men.

• Eating cattle sacred to Helios, the sun god, when stranded on the island of Thrinacia. Enraged, Helios persuaded Zeus to send a terrible storm, which sank the last ship. All but Odysseus perished.

• Being rescued by the sea nymph Calypso, who fell in love with him and kept him prisoner on her island for seven years.

• Being shipwrecked, after his release, by a storm sent by Poseidon. Washed up on the island of Scheria, he was rescued by the nymph Nausicaa, whose father, King Alcinous, recognized him and provided a new vessel, which carried him home.

• Making landfall back on Ithaca to find his wife Penelope besieged by suitors who thought him dead. He disguised himself as a beggar to confront and kill his rivals, before reclaiming his role as Penelope's husband and the island's ruler.

... THE EIGHT DYNAMICS ...
OF SCIENTOLOGY

Founded in 1952 by science-fiction writer **Lafayette (L.) Ron Hubbard** (1911–1986), Scientology teaches that the energizing principle of existence is survival, subdivided into eight areas or "dynamics", which are represented by the eight arms of the Scientology cross. By understanding these dynamics and their relationship with one other, Scientologists believe they can extend themselves spiritually. Each of us is essentially an immortal alien spirit ("thetan").

1. ***Self:*** the urge to survive as an individual.

2. ***Creativity:*** the urge to procreate, have children, and raise and nurture future generations.

3. ***Groups:*** the urge for communal survival, whether in a social group, political party, church or nation.

4. ***Mankind:*** the urge for all peoples of the world to move forward as a species.

5. ***All living things:*** the urge for all life forms to survive and flourish.

6. ***Physical universe:*** the urge for the survival of the entire cosmos (made up of matter, energy, space and time, or MEST).

7. ***Spirituality:*** the urge to survive and grow as spiritual beings.

8. ***Infinity, or Supreme Being:*** the urge toward existence as infinity, the "allness of all".

• THE HOME HERBAL FIRST-AID KIT •

Herbs can provide gentle and effective alternatives to standard medicines. The following basic remedies are useful to have in any home:

REMEDY	PROPERTIES	PRACTICAL APPLICATIONS
Aloe vera gel	Soothing, cooling, antifungal	Minor burns, scalds, sunburn; fungal infections, wounds, insect bites
Calendula cream	Antiseptic, antifungal	Cuts, grazes and sore, broken skin
Chickweed cream	Astringent, anti-rheumatic, heals wounds	Boils, burns, scalds; insect stings and splinters; eczema and rheumatism
Chamomile tea	Soothing, calming	Shock and nervous upsets
Comfrey ointment	Astringent, heals wounds	Bruises, sprains, inflamed bunions, arthritis
Peppermint powder/tea	Digestive tonic, carminative, antispasmodic	Upset stomach, travel sickness, nausea, headaches
Witch hazel (distilled)	Astringent, soothing	Burns, sunburn, insect bites; bruises and sprains (make ice cubes)

• ASPECTS OF THE MEDICINE WHEEL •

The Medicine Wheel, an interpretation of Native American shamanism, is a ring of 36 stones – each representing a totem animal or divine source of energy (Father Sun, Mother Earth and so on). By meditating on the wheel and its symbols (see below for those relating to the four cardinal directions), we can gain a deeper understanding of creation, and our own place within it:

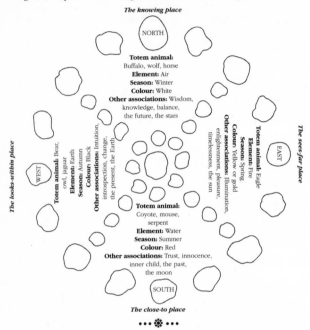

The knowing place

NORTH

Totem animal: Buffalo, wolf, horse
Element: Air
Season: Winter
Colour: White
Other associations: Wisdom, knowledge, balance, the future, the stars

The looks-within place

WEST

Totem animal: Bear, owl, jaguar
Element: Earth
Season: Autumn
Colour: Black
Other associations: Intuition, introspection, change, the present, the Earth

The sees-far place

EAST

Totem animal: Eagle
Element: Fire
Season: Spring
Colour: Yellow or gold
Other associations: Illumination, enlightenment, pleasure, timelessness, the sun

Totem animal: Coyote, mouse, serpent
Element: Water
Season: Summer
Colour: Red
Other associations: Trust, innocence, inner child, the past, the moon

SOUTH

The close-to place

• • • HOW TO PRACTISE CAODAI • • •

In CaoDai, a universal faith founded in Vietnam in 1926, the ultimate goal is to be reunified with "The All That Is". Here's how to work toward this:

• Practise good and avoid evil.

• Show kindness to nature, plants, animals and human beings.

• Adopt vegetarianism for at least ten days per month (for self-purification and love).

• Worship the Supreme Being in four daily ceremonies (6am, noon, 6pm, midnight).

• Complete duties toward yourself, your family, society, country, all living beings and nature.

• Meditate to develop the divine within.

• • • SIX FAMOUS GIANTS • • •

Argus *(Greek myth):* Thought never to slumber as some of his 100 eyes always remained open. Therefore employed by Zeus's wife Hera to watch over the nymph Io (whom her husband coveted). But Zeus sent for the music god Hermes, who made Argus drowsy and killed him with a stone.

Polyphemus *(Greek myth):* Son of the sea god Poseidon. Had a single vast eye in the middle of his forehead. Blinded by Odysseus and his crew after keeping them captive on their return from Troy *(see p98).*

Geryon *(Greek myth):* Grandson of the Gorgon Medusa. Three-headed, three-bodied and six-armed. Met his end at the hands of Herakles *(see p37).*

Goliath *(Bible):* Fought for the Philistines against the Israelites. Remembered for his battle with David, future king of Israel (1 Samuel 17): David first stunned him with a stone from his slingshot and then beheaded him with Goliath's own sword.

Geirrod *(Norse myth):* Sought to lure Thor, god of thunder, to his castle, unprotected by his magical belt and hammer. Forewarned and forearmed, Thor killed him, together with his entourage of frost giants.

Hrungnir *(Norse myth):* Killed by Thor after finding his way to Asgard, the realm of the gods, and drunkenly boasting of his intention to abduct the goddesses Sif and Freyja.

••• ❂ •••

• • • HOW TO PERFORM • • • THE WHISPERED "AH"

The actor **Frederick Matthias Alexander** (1869–1955) developed the Alexander Technique as a means of self-help when he started to lose his voice during performances – it turned out he had chronic laryngitis. Understanding that most people (himself included) tend to use breaths that are too fast and shallow, he developed an exercise called the Whispered "Ah", which aimed to lengthen and deepen the breath, maximize use of the lungs and strengthen the voice. It's of particular benefit for public speakers, but also soothes anxiety and insomnia.

1: Blow air gently out through your mouth (without stiffening your neck). Allow the air to return naturally through your nose. Repeat.

2: Think of something that makes you smile and place the tip of your tongue against the back of your lower teeth.

3: Allow your jaw to drop forward and down, and whisper "Ah" on the out-breath.

4: Close your mouth as the breath ends, allowing the air to come back in through your nose.

5: Repeat the whole procedure three or four times.

• HINDU DEITIES AND THEIR VEHICLES •

The many gods and goddesses of Hinduism, including the triad (*trimurti*) of supreme divinities, Shiva, Vishnu and Brahma, are carried by animal mounts, or "vehicles" (*vahanas*). As well as providing transport for its respective deity, each creature acts as a loyal messenger, relaying prayers to the god and returning divine grace to the supplicant.

DIVINITY	VEHICLE	ASSOCIATIONS	
Shiva supreme god; the destroyer or transformer	Nandi, a snow-white bull	Power, primal strength, sexual energy	
Vishnu supreme god; the preserver	Garuda, a golden bird-man	Control of thoughts, balance of good and evil	
Brahma god of creation	Hamsa, the water bird (a goose or swan)	Grace, beauty, peace, discrimination, enlightenment	
Saraswati consort of Brahma	Peacock	Arrogance, pride, the arts	
Durga/Kali warrior aspect of the divine mother	Lion	Cruelty, anger, pride, mercilessness	
Ganesha elephant-headed god	Mouse or rat	Wisdom, the removal of obstacles	

DIVINITY	VEHICLE	ASSOCIATIONS	
Lakshmi consort of Vishnu	Owl	Wisdom, emergence from ignorance	
Indra god of war and weather, supreme deity in Vedic times	Airavata, the elephant	Fortitude, courage	

••• ✺ •••

• FOUR TAROT DECKS •

A collection of seventeen cards seems to have been made for Charles VI of France as early as 1392, and it was shortly afterwards (1415) that the Major Arcana (*see p131*) first made an appearance. Italian designs predominated in the Tarot until the 18th century. Here are some landmark decks:

Visconti-Sforza Tarot *(1400s):* Oldest known deck, commissioned by the Duke of Milan, Filippo Maria Visconti (reflecting the aristocratic vogue of the time for card games). Various versions, decorated with gold, exist in fragmentary forms across Europe, but none contains a full set of the Major Arcana as we know them today.

Tarot of Marseilles *(c.1499):* Influential deck that established the 22 Major Arcana. In the 16th century, when the Tarot was mainly used for games of chance rather than divination or self-development, this deck became a standard. Influences all later Tarot decks. Its replacement of the High Priestess card with the image of a female pope was viewed by some as a satirical swipe at Catholicism.

Rider-Waite Tarot *(1909):* Richly symbolic deck that renewed interest in the Tarot in the modern age. A.E. Waite, member of the occult Order of the Golden Dawn, created it as an accompaniment to his Tarot-based writings. He highlighted the universal nature of the Tarot by removing many of the Christian elements present in earlier decks.

Thoth Tarot *(1943):* Occult interpretation by Aleister Crowley, who was associated with the black arts and developed designs in line with his systems of "magick" – for example, Strength was changed to Lust in Crowley's deck, in accord with his beliefs in "sexual magick". Theories about the Tarot's origins in Egypt are also manifested in his designs, which include sphinx and ankh motifs.

• YOGIC ENERGY AND ITS CHANNELS •

The Sanskrit word *prana* refers to the universal life-force, or energy, inside every living thing. It circulates in the human body via a network of 72,000 invisible channels called *nadis*. The more smoothly *prana* flows through the *nadis*, the better one's state of overall health. An even flow can be promoted by breathing exercises, meditation and yoga asanas. The three most important of the many nadis are *sushumna*, *ida* and *pingala*:

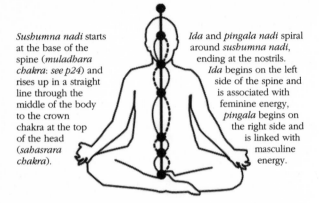

Sushumna nadi starts at the base of the spine (*muladhara chakra: see p24*) and rises up in a straight line through the middle of the body to the crown chakra at the top of the head (*sahasrara chakra*).

Ida and *pingala nadi* spiral around *sushumna nadi*, ending at the nostrils. *Ida* begins on the left side of the spine and is associated with feminine energy, *pingala* begins on the right side and is linked with masculine energy.

At the base *of sushumna nadi* lies a dormant source of transformative energy, *kundalini*. Committed yoga practice can awaken this energy and draw it up the *sushumna nadi*. If it reaches the crown chakra, the result is *samadhi*, a state of self-realization, where ego ceases to exist. However, it's best to initiate this with the guidance of a teacher, as kundalini rising too fast can cause strong mental and physical reactions.

••• ❀ •••

• • • SCHOOLS OF BUDDHISM • • •

Shortly after the Buddha's death, a council of monks met to establish the official Buddhist doctrine. Within 300 years of this event, 18 different schools of thought had arisen. The doctrinal debate was frequently sharp, but in fact Buddhists of different schools often inhabited the same monasteries, and today it is easy to assume that these early divisions were more serious than they were. Two main groups, or vehicles, emerged over the centuries (the term "vehicle" relates to the idea of a ferryboat that crosses the "sea of *samsara*", or suffering, to nirvana).

• **Hinayana** ("small vehicle"), whose monks aimed to reach nirvana by achieving the status of *arhat* ("worthy and enlightened one"). Today's surviving branch of Hinayana is known as **Theravada** ("what the elders said"), which is practised in Sri Lanka, Myanmar, Thailand and other parts of SE Asia. The secret of Theravada's longevity arguably results from three different factors: its strict adherence to the letter of the Pali scriptures (*see p67*); its flair for creating strong monastic institutions and for sustaining ties with secular government; and its flexibility in co-existing with and absorbing elements of non-Buddhist folk religion.

• **Mahayana** ("greater vehicle"), whose schools variously believed that everyone can achieve nirvana, either through enlightenment or by the intervention of a spiritual being termed a *bodhisattva* (*see p51*). Buddhism had become eradicated in India by the 15th century, but Mahayana was established in Tibet, Nepal, China and Japan. The main Mahayana schools today are Zen, Pure Land, Nichiren Buddhism, Shingon, Tibetan Buddhism and Tendai. The present Dalai Lama, exiled from Tibet, is perhaps the world's most famous (Mahayana) Buddhist ever.

••• ❁ •••

• • QIGONG: WU CHI • •

The Chinese term *qigong* means "energy exercises". The postures and movements of *qigong* promote the free flow of vital energy (*qi*) in the body, stimulate the internal organs and deepen breathing.

The basic *qigong* standing posture is called *wu chi* (meaning "emptiness") and not only enhances body awareness, but is an effective stress-buster. Try to stay relaxed throughout and perform the exercise with calm awareness:

1. Stand with your feet shoulder-width apart. Find your natural balance – leaning neither too far forward nor too far back. Now hang your arms loosely by your sides.

2. Feel your heels, your little toes and your big toes all relaxed on the ground.

3. Allow your knees to bend a little but make sure they don't move further forward than your toes.

4. Relax your lower back, your stomach and your buttocks.

5. Relax and slightly round your shoulders to let your chest feel "hollow".

6. Imagine that a string is attached to the top of your head and that someone is gently pulling it upward, and you with it. Relax your tongue, mouth and jaw.

7. Remain in this posture, breathing fully but gently – in through your nose and out through your mouth. Take your mind through the five elements:

Earth: feel grounded and rooted
Water: feel loose and fluid
Air: feel light and transparent
Fire: feel sparkly and fun
Space: feel the space within each joint and muscle, and between each breath and thought

8. Relax for a few minutes, before resuming normal activities.

THE SYMBOLISM OF
• • • NATIVE AMERICAN • • •
TOTEM ANIMALS

Native Americans believe that animal spirits, or totems, can reveal enlightening messages to anyone willing to pay attention. If a certain animal appears to you frequently, in your dreams, thoughts or perceptions, it's worth considering its meaning. The symbolism of some creatures, such as gentle deer, far-sighted eagle or loyal dog, will no doubt seem obvious. Here are some less obvious creatures and their best-known associations:

Ant
patience, perseverance, organization, willingness to work for the good of all, selflessness

Badger
aggression, courage, strength, willingness to fight for what is necessary, keeper of stories

Bat
death and rebirth, letting go of the old to embrace the new, initiation

Butterfly
transformation, regeneration, life, beauty, change, fear of stagnation

Frog
fertility, regeneration, happiness, transformation, cleansing

Mouse
caution, scrutiny, organization, a need to see the larger picture

Otter
joy, female energy, curiosity, adventure, playfulness, courage, constancy

Porcupine
sensitivity, tenderness, trust, innocence, humility, faith, family, defence

Rabbit
community, abundance, fertility, vigilance, cowardice, overcoming fear

Raven
magic, sorcery, prediction, shape-shifting, the power of the unknown, the void

Spider
creation, female energy, sex and death, fate, entrapment, warning of becoming entangled

Woodpecker
thunderstorms, invisibility, Mother Earth, the rains

... A SHORT HISTORY ...
OF CROP CIRCLES

More than 12,000 crop circles have been identified, mostly in southern England. Explanations range from freak meteorological occurrences (such as ball lightning) and military experiments to UFO landings and extraterrestrial communication. Many are known to be hoaxes. Students of crop circles are called cerealogists, or "croppies". Some cerealogists believe that in genuine crop circles the stems are bent in a way that could never be achieved by human manipulation.

815CE: The first known mention of crop circles, in a letter from the Bishop of Lyons, France, to a priest, warning him of crops flattened by "magic storms".

1678: A woodcut pamphlet called *The Mowing Devil* printed in Hertfordshire, England, illustrates a tailed creature scything a circular pattern in a cornfield. This relates to the story of a farmer who, after telling an expensive labourer that he would rather pay the Devil to do the work, found next morning that his crops had been "so neatly mow'd by the Devil or some Infernal Spirit, that no Mortal Man was able to do the like".

1880: The science journal *Nature* reports on a field of crop circles in Surrey, England, suggesting they were caused by "cyclonic wind action".

1966: A farmer in Queensland, Australia, witnesses a UFO rise from a swamp, near the town of Tully. At the site of lift-off he finds a swirled, round mat of reeds floating on water, among the growing reed-stems.

1978–1990 Large numbers of crop circles appear in southern England – initially simple circles, circles with accompanying rings, and Celtic cross variations; later, more complex pictograms, with straight lines.

1990s: Larger, even more complex designs appear in southern England, some with fractals or based on advanced mathematics.

1991: Two Englishmen, Doug Bower and Dave Chorley, admit to faking more than 200 crop circles since 1978; Bower reveals their technique on TV. To what extent these hoaxers inspired others remains an unresolved question.

1992: Two Hungarian teenagers are sued for damages in connection with a hoax crop circle they created 40 miles (64km) west of Budapest. The circle had been pronounced genuine by numerous experts.

2002: Discovery Channel shows a TV program featuring students from MIT (Massachusetts Institute of Technology) commissioned to create a crop circle in Ohio. Opinion differs as to whether the result was convincingly "authentic" when judged by scientific tests.

⊹⇌ ❋ ⇌⊹

• • • *FOOD LAWS* • • •

Most religions have dietary rules – eg Judaism and Islam have a strong prohibition against consuming blood. Here is a simplified overview:

	BUDDHISM	CHRISTIANITY	HINDUISM	JUDAISM	ISLAM
Alcohol	✗	✓	✗	✓ if kosher*	✗
Animal fat	✗	✓	✓ (not all Hindus)	✓ if kosher*	✗
Eggs	✓	✓	✓ (not all Hindus)	✓ if no embryo	✓ if no embryo
Dairy produce	✓	✓	✗ if made with animal rennet	✗ if made with animal rennet, or within 3 hours of eating meat	✗ if made with animal rennet
Fish	✗ (not all Buddhists)	✓	✓ if it has fins/scales	✓ if it has fins/scales and a backbone	✓
Shellfish	✗	✓	✓ (not all Hindus)	✗	✓
Chicken	✗	✓	✗	✓ if kosher*	✓ if halal**
Lamb	✗	✓	✗	✓ if kosher*	✓ if halal**
Beef	✗	✓	✗	✓ if kosher*	✓ if halal**
Pork	✗	✓	✗	✗	✗

* *kosher*: permissible according to Jewish dietary law (*kashrut*), derived mainly from the books of Leviticus and Deuteronomy, the Misnah and the Talmud.
** *halal*: permissible under Islamic law, as prescribed by the Qur'an; the term also applies to other areas of life, such as clothing and conduct.

• • *ZEN BUDDHISM IN SHORT* • •

• The earliest form of Zen was brought to China in the 6th century BCE, by the Indian monk Bodhidharma, and was originally called *Chan* Buddhism. From there it spread to Korea, Japan and other parts of Asia.
• Zen practice consists mainly of seated meditation (*zazen*). This calms the body and mind, and encourages direct insight into the nature of existence.
• The two main Japanese schools of Zen are Rinzai and Soto.
• Poetry, painting, calligraphy, ceramics, flower arranging, gardening, cookery, archery and swordsmanship are all traditional Zen practices, encouraging mindfulness in daily experience.

• • • THE POWER OF COLOUR • • •

Colour has been used therapeutically for millennia. Modern research has confirmed the principles of colour therapy – the idea that colour can bring about measurable emotional and physical changes in our make-up. Here are some recent findings of interest:

Viewing **red** can increase heart rate and blood pressure.

High blood pressure can be lowered by visualizing **blue**.

People will be more sociable in a room painted **yellow**.

Painting the bathroom **orange**, **pink** or **yellow** can alleviate constipation.

In prison, walls painted **pink** make inmates quieter.

Violet can combat depression.

People who wear a lot of **royal blue** find it harder to lose weight.

Indigo can help with tensions, nosebleeds, insomnia, neuralgia.

A **black** business suit can seem intimidating.

• • • SOME UNUSUAL FORMS • • • OF DIVINATION

Alectoromancy: Reading the letters revealed as a cockerel eats the kernels of corn that cover them **Belomancy:** Picking out arrows from a quiver, where each arrow has had marks or words written on it **Bibliomancy:** Opening books at random and reading the first passage seen, especially from sacred texts such as the Bible **Cledonomancy:** Paying attention to and interpreting chance events or the remarks of passers-by **Cleromancy:** Sorting or casting lots, dice or bones **Extispicy (also known as haruspicy):** Inspecting animal entrails for anomalies **Hydromancy:** Looking for signs, such as ripples, on the surface of water **Moleosophy:** Reading moles on the body – shape, size, colour and placement are all considered **Myomancy:** Observing the movement and behaviour of mice **Necromancy:** Calling up the spirits of the dead, generally associated in the West with black magic **Oneiromancy:** Interpreting dreams **Onychomancy:** Reading symbols formed by the reflection of sunlight on the oiled fingernails of a child **Pyromancy:** Observing the shape of a flame or flames, or burning something and interpreting the result **Tasseomancy:** "Reading" the patterns of tea leaves, coffee grounds or wine sediments left at the bottom of a cup or a glass.

• • • SELF-SHIATSU • • •

Shiatsu combines two Japanese words: *shi* ("finger") and *atsu* ("pressure"). Performing "finger-pressure" massage on your own head and face is a great way to stimulate vital meridians (energy pathways; *see p68*) and encourage *ki* (vital energy) to flow more freely, boosting overall vitality. This facial workout makes a great wakeup routine for the mornings:

1. Keeping your wrists loose, tap with your fingers all over the top of your head – to stimulate the brain.

2. Place your hands across your forehead so that your fingertips meet in the centre. Slowly smooth your fingers out toward the temples, then circle your fingertips here – both sides at the same time.

3. Squeeze along your eyebrows with the thumb and index finger of each hand. Then press gently but firmly around your eye sockets with your fingertips.

4. Rub your cheeks and the end of your nose to boost circulation.

5. Use your thumbs to press into the pressure points, or *tsubos,* just beneath the outside corners of your nostrils. Then use your thumbs to massage across your face to your ears – to help nasal congestion and stuffy sinuses.

6. Pull your ear-lobes, then rub all over your ears to further boost circulation.

7. Pinch along your lower jaw to help to release toxins.

••• ✹ •••

• • • THE SRI YANTRA • • •

A yantra is a geometric representation of the universe used by Hindu Tantric adepts as a focus for meditation. It is the yogic equivalent of a Buddhist mandala.

One of the most renowned types is the *Sri yantra* (shown here), containing nine interlocking triangles within a border of concentric circles. The four upward-pointing triangles symbolize Shiva, or masculine energy; while the five downward-pointing ones represent Shakti, or feminine energy. The interplay of the two is the energy of creation. The complex pattern made by the triangles in their interaction with each other, yielding 43 smaller triangles, is a symbol of the harmonious cosmos. The inner circle enclosing the triangles is embellished by the petals of an eight-petalled lotus; beyond that there is a sixteen-petalled lotus; and finally a square, with four protrusions symbolizing the doors of a temple.

The design is arranged in a way that draws the meditator's awareness toward the still point (*bindu*) in the centre. This inward movement represents spiritual progress on the path to enlightenment.

✦ THE CHINESE ZODIAC AT A GLANCE ✦

In Chinese astrology, which is based on the twelve-year cycle of the Chinese lunar calendar, the timing of your birth determines which of the twelve traditional zodiac animals influences your character, and in what way:

• Your birth *year* determines your *outer* animal – the qualities that you most readily display to the world.

• Your birth *month* determines your *inner* animal – the characteristics and motivations that lie behind your actions.

• Your birth *hour* determines your *secret* animal – the very core of your character, which the rest of the world rarely gets to see.

BIRTH YEAR*	BIRTH MONTH	BIRTH HOUR	ANIMAL	QUALITIES
1924, 1936, 1948, 1960, 1972, 1984, 1996, 2008	December 7–January 5	23:00–1:00	Rat	Eloquent, charming, disciplined; can be ruthless
1925, 1937, 1949, 1961, 1973, 1985, 1997, 2009	January 6–February 3	01:00–3:00	Ox	Calm, hardworking, dependable; can be stubborn
1926, 1938, 1950, 1962, 1974, 1986, 1998, 2010	February 4–March 5	3:00–5:00	Tiger	Rebellious, powerful, passionate, generous; can be reckless and irritable
1927, 1939, 1951, 1963, 1975, 1987, 1999, 2011	March 6–April 4	5:00–7:00	Rabbit	Sensitive, compassionate, flexibile, cautious; can be detached and brooding
1928, 1940, 1952, 1964, 1976, 1988, 2000, 2012	April 5–May 4	7:00–9:00	Dragon	Dignified, passionate, decisive; can be arrogant and impetuous.
1929, 1941 1953, 1965, 1977, 1989, 2001, 2013	May 5–June 5	9:00–11:00	Snake	Profound, prudent, sensual, creative, durable; can be possessive and distrustful
1930, 1942, 1954, 1966, 1978, 1990, 2002, 2014	June 6–July 6	11:00–13:00	Horse	Perceptive, cheerful, popular intelligent; can be unstable
1931, 1943, 1955, 1967, 1979, 1991, 2003, 2015	July 7–August 6	13:00-15:00	Sheep	Gentle sympathetic; can be pessimistic and over-sensitive
1932, 1944, 1956, 1968, 1980, 1992, 2004, 2016	August 7–September 7	15:00-17:00	Monkey	Quick-witted, inquisitive, sociable; can be egocentric, impatient and jealous
1933, 1945, 1957, 1969, 1981, 1993, 2005, 2017	September 8–October 7	17:00–19:00	Rooster	Self-assured, decisive, practical; can be critical and opinionated
1934, 1946, 1958, 1970, 1982, 1994, 2006, 2018	October 8–November 6	19:00–21:00	Dog	Loyal, honest, practical, amiable; can be cynical
1935, 1947, 1959, 1971, 1983, 1995, 2007, 2019	November 7–December 6	21:00–23:00	Pig	Honest, patient, understanding, loyal; can be naïve and self-indulgent

*Years are given according to the Chinese sexegenary calendar. If your birthday is in January or February, check against a Chinese calendar whether you actually fall within the previous Chinese year.

• *THE SIX PRINCIPLES OF PILATES* •

Pilates, developed by Joseph Pilates in the early 20th century, tones and conditions, improving posture and increasing flexibility. It lengthens and strengthens the body, eases stress and tension and helps you become more graceful in your movement. It also alleviates back pain. Six fundamental principles underpin every Pilates exercise:

Breathing: Breathing deeply, expanding the chest and ribs, is key: you breathe in to prepare for a movement, breathe out as you move, and breathe in to recover.

Control: Movements are slow, controlled, meditative, the mind constantly focused on using the correct body part for each exercise.

Coordination: The aim is to re-establish effective communication between brain and body.

Centering: Each movement is done from the "core" – drawing the abdominal muscles in and up, from navel to spine (to strengthen the back and flatten the stomach).

Flow: All movements are done in a smooth, slow way, avoiding anything jerky or hurried.

Precision: Conscious awareness helps the central nervous system to choose precisely the right muscles for each movement.

• *FIVE CHANNELLED BEINGS* • *AND THEIR TEACHINGS*

Channelling happens when a person goes into a trance-state and receives information from a higher being, or from their own higher consciousness. This may include basic guidance on the profound truths of existence. Below are some notable examples:

HIGHER BEING	CHANNELLED BY	DESCRIPTION OF HIGHER BEING	KEY MESSAGE RECEIVED
Ramtha	J.Z. Knight (b.1946)	35,000-year-old warrior king who conquered Atlantis	"What be you? You be God"
Seth	Jane Roberts (1929–1984)	"energy personality essence"	"You create your experience through your beliefs in yourself"
Lazaris	Jach Pursel (b.1947)	"spark of consciousness"	"Take full and total responsibility for your reality"
"Jesus"	Helen Schucman (1909–1981)	"spirit Jesus"	"All is God: God is all" and "Fear is an illusion"
Emmanuel	Pat Rodegast (b.1926)	"you without your fear"	"Every moment of your life you are offered the opportunity to choose – love or fear"

• THE KABBALISTIC TREE OF LIFE •

A complex symbol of both the universe (macrocosm) and humankind (microcosm), the Tree of Life is a profound spiritual diagram used by Kabbalists in mystical Judaism as well as in Western mystery tradition.

The tree contains ten *sephiroth* (singular: *sephira*), or qualities of God – the emanations by which God can make Himself known to humankind. The *sephirot* are differentiated into "the Pillar of Severity" (feminine energy) and "the Pillar of Mercy" (masculine energy). There are many attributes connected with each *sephira* and also with the paths that connect them. Kabbalists practise meditations by which they start in *Malkuth* and travel upward in ever-deepening mystical experience. The labels at the sides of the tree list, in order, the name of God and part of the body associated with each *sephira*.

The Pillar of Equilibrium

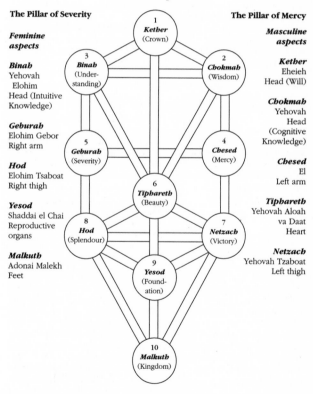

The Pillar of Severity

Feminine aspects

Binah
Yehovah
Elohim
Head (Intuitive
Knowledge)

Geburah
Elohim Gebor
Right arm

Hod
Elohim Tsaboat
Right thigh

Yesod
Shaddai el Chai
Reproductive
organs

Malkuth
Adonai Malekh
Feet

The Pillar of Mercy

Masculine aspects

Kether
Eheieh
Head (Will)

Chokmah
Yehovah
Head
(Cognitive
Knowledge)

Chesed
El
Left arm

Tiphareth
Yehovah Aloah
va Daat
Heart

Netzach
Yehovah Tzaboat
Left thigh

(Diagram circles:)
1 **Kether** (Crown)
3 **Binah** (Under-standing)
2 **Chokmah** (Wisdom)
5 **Geburah** (Severity)
4 **Chesed** (Mercy)
6 **Tiphareth** (Beauty)
8 **Hod** (Splendour)
7 **Netzach** (Victory)
9 **Yesod** (Found-ation)
10 **Malkuth** (Kingdom)

• • • JUNG'S DREAM ARCHETYPES • • •

The pioneering Swiss psychologist **Carl Jung** (1875–1961) identified universal figures he termed "archetypes", which may emerge from the collective unconscious (*see p59*) in our dreams. He believed that they are most likely to appear to us at times of major change or uncertainty. Interpreting them once they are recognized can help us to find our "true selves", for they tend to embody aspects of our innermost nature. Some of the most significant archetypes are listed below:

The Wise Old Man may be a teacher, magician or other authority figure. Represents a primal source of wisdom.

The Hero can present itself in any positive form. Symbolizes our questing side that seeks to do good and to find answers to life's fundamental questions.

The Trickster often appears as some sort of clown who mocks the pretensions of the ego. Makes us review, and perhaps change, established ways of thinking.

The Persona often appears as a vaguely familiar stranger. Represents the mask we adopt to present ourselves to the outside world. It shouldn't be mistaken our real self.

The Shadow often emerges in a threatening role. Represents the primitive side of ourselves that can be hard to accept. Acknowledging the Shadow can help us to transform some of its negative aspects into positive.

The Divine Child usually appears as an infant. Symbolizes the true self, the dawn of new opportunities and a desire for wholeness. Also reminds us how far we have strayed from our original identity.

The Anima represents intuitive "feminine" qualities, often neglected by men; **the Animus** represents "masculine" qualities, such as assertiveness and courage, that women can find within themselves.

• • • HOW TO PRACTISE • • •
MINDFULNESS

Mindfulness can be described as meditation pared of any spiritual connotations. At its most basic, it simply involves stopping and becoming thoroughly aware of the sensations of the moment as often as possible, gently letting go of any stray worries or thoughts that may cross the mind.

The practice was first advocated in the West by scientist **Jon Kabat-Zinn** (b.1944), who was looking for a way to help people to kick-start their own healing powers. He found that mindfulness could help to ease anxiety and depression, and relieve pain. It has since been used to deal with a huge range of physical and psychological ailments.

Kabat-Zinn encourages his patients to aim for 45 minutes of practice a day, focusing on the breath alone. However, he advises that even a few minutes a day can boost well-being. Here are a few ways to introduce the practice into your everyday routine:

• Tune into the ordinary details of your daily life: the feeling of the water hitting your body in the shower; the taste of every bite of your food; the colours and smells of the world around you.

• Once in a while throughout the day, stop, sit down and become aware of your breathing. Breathe deeply and slowly, and let go of everything else. Allow yourself to be exactly who you are.

• Get down on the floor and do some mindful stretching exercises now and again, if only for a few minutes. Stay in touch with your breathing. What is your body telling you?

• • • THE AYURVEDIC DOSHAS • • •

Ayurveda, the traditional system of medicine native to India, teaches that everyone has a basic nature (*prakruti*) dominated by one of the three *doshas*, or humours: *vata* (ether and air), *pitta* (fire) or *kapha* (earth and water). By knowing which *dosha* dominates your *prakruti*, and adjusting your diet and lifestyle to suit, you can help to maintain good health. Use the information below to assess this:

	VATA	PITTA	KAPHA
Characteristics	Slim and fine-boned; fast and agile; feels the cold; fearful, highly strung, imaginative; prominent veins	Medium build; hot, red face; freckles and moles; sensitive to heat, hunger and thirst; intolerant, competitive; good leadership qualities	Large, solid frame; soft, clear skin; sensible, placid, even-tempered; can easily skip meals; slow and measured lifestyle; good endurance
How to tell if out of balance	Dry skin, dryness in mouth, fatigue, giddiness, stiffness, pain, lack of appetite, hiccups, insomnia	Body odour, excess perspiration, rashes or acne, herpes, inflammation, anger and irritation, burning sensations, heartburn	Heaviness in body, excess salivation, sweet taste in mouth, drowsiness, feeling cold, nausea, itchy feeling in throat, depression, weight gain
How to treat if out of balance	Sweet, sour and hot foods; massages with certain oils; rest, relaxation and sleep; enemas; routine; laughter	Sweet, bitter, astringent and cool foods; fasting (*see p35*); cool baths and massages; consolation and comfort	Pungent, bitter, astringent and sharp foods; hot baths and steam treatments; vigorous exercise; lots of action and new activities

... KEY BELIEFS AND PRACTICES ... FROM NATIVE NORTH AMERICA

Emergence of the Tribe: A creation myth according to which ancestors reached the present world by climbing through underground layers, to emerge from a hole known as the "earth's navel".

Sun Dance: A celebration of creation, with feasting and dancing lasting several days; thanks are offered, with prayers for renewal and health. Normally performed at the summer solstice.

Sweat Lodges: Constructed from wood, animal skins and heated rocks, these structures generate moist, hot air, like a sauna, and are entered for purification, spiritual renewal and healing.

Vision Quest: A ritual undertaken by boys at puberty, involving fasting alone in the wilderness to encounter a vision and a guardian spirit.

Snake Dance: A ceremony performed with live snakes between the dancer's teeth, believed to petition the nature gods to bring rain.

Hunting Ceremonies: Rituals honouring animals after they have been killed, in order to appease their spirits and express gratitude for the success of the hunt.

	NAVAJO	HOPI	SIOUX	APACHE	COMANCHE	HURON	CHEROKEE
Emergence of the Tribe	•	•		•			
Sun Dance	•		•	•	•		•
Sweat Lodges	•		•	•	•	•	
Vision Quest			•	•	•		•
Snake Dance		•					
Hunting Ceremonies		•	•			•	

••• 🕸 •••

• BAHA'I: THE ALL-EMBRACING FAITH •

Founded in 1863, Baha'i is one of the youngest major religions. Its central tenet is spiritual unity. Unusually, devotees accept the validity of all other faiths, viewing such teachers as Moses, Jesus Christ, Zoroaster, the Buddha, Krishna and Mohammed as divine messengers or "manifestations" sent by God, each reflecting a single divine truth like mirrors held up to the sun from different places. Each manifestation is believed to have played an important part in teaching moral and spiritual values, therefore helping to advance civilization by "progressive revelation".

The founder of Baha'i was **Baha'u'llah** (1817–1892), son of a prominent Persian governor in Tehran. He became a supporter of Sayyid Ali Muhammad Shirazi (1819–1850), who called himself **the Bab** ("Gate")

– a young preacher of unity who claimed to be a messenger from God. The Bab's teachings were seen as a threat by Iran's Shi'ite clergy, who had him executed in 1850. Before his death, he prophesied that a greater messenger would appear – Baha'u'llah is believed to be this person.

Baha'u'llah rejected the wealth and privilege of his family, instead preaching his message of equality throughout Iran and the Ottoman Empire. He suffered imprisonment, banishment and assassination attempts as a result of ideas expressed in several books, including *Kalimat-i-Maknunih* (The Hidden Words), *Kitab-i-Quan* (The Book of Certitude) *and Kitab-i-Aqdas* (The Book of Laws). After his death he was succeeded by his son Abdu'l-Baha (1844–1921).

Today, there are some six million Baha'is, in more than 200 countries. They are administrated by nine elected members of the Universal House of Justice, based in Haifa, Israel. Anyone can become a Baha'i without having to renounce their own religion.

••• ✿ •••

• *HOW TO CONDUCT A HOME SÉANCE* •

A talking board, or Ouija board, with a planchette (sliding indicator), was a popular way to attempt contact with deceased souls in the 19th century. The first Ouija board patent was filed on February 10 1891 in the USA. Some psychologists argue that the device can cause severe mental problems; some Christians say that it's a portal for demonic possession. Here's how to make and use an improvised version:

1. Write the letters of the alphabet and the numbers 0 to 10 on 36 small square pieces of card. Also write YES and NO on separate cards.

2. Sit at a table, with at least one other person, and lay a large piece of paper or board over it. Place YES at the top and NO at the bottom. Position an upturned glass in the centre.

3. Lay the letters in a circle, starting with A to the right of YES. Continue clockwise until Z is at the other side of YES.

4. Place the numbers at the bottom, beneath the NO. Secure all the cards to the paper or board with adhesive.

5. Each person should place one finger on the upturned glass. There's no need to press hard.

6. One person should ask the question: "Is there a spirit present?" (or words to that effect). If the glass moves to the word YES, get ready to speak with the spirit.

7. Ask any questions you have in mind for the deceased. It's important for only one person to ask a question at a time. Keep a sheet of paper at hand to write down any letters as they are spelled out in response, as well as any numbers that are given in answer to date questions. It can help to have an "extra" person to write down the answers.

8. Answers sometimes come in foreign languages; words may be spelled backwards. Some imaginative interpretation may be needed to yield a clear message.

... SEVEN MARRIAGE CUSTOMS ...
FROM AROUND THE WORLD

The Amish
Weddings are held after the harvest (reflecting the intensely practical approach of the Amish). The bride wears a blue dress that will be worn again at important events in her life. Church rules forbid personal adornment, so she wears no jewelry. The ceremony takes place over several hours, with a feast and storytelling. The newly-weds spend their first night at the bride's parents' house.

Mormonism *(the Jesus Christ Church of the Latter Day Saints)*
Couples are "sealed" as husband and wife for all eternity – in a "celestial marriage". Only those who are "temple-recommended" are allowed to witness the ceremony (causing controversy, as this excludes non-Mormon friends and relatives of the couple). Fundamentalist Mormons still believe in polygamy, although it was officially abandoned in 1890 and is now condemned by the central Mormon Church.

The Unification Church *(also known as the Moonies, after its founder Sun Myung Moon)*
The Church holds mass ceremonies (often in stadiums), in which hundreds or even thousands of couples are wedded simultaneously. These arranged marriages join people from different countries and cultures, many of whom have only very recently met – all part of the church's declared attempt to unite people from all over the world.

Wicca
Marriage involves the age-old tradition of "hand-fasting": the couple's hands are fastened together with cord or ribbon. This signifies their union and is the origin of the term "to tie the knot". Some couples also jump over a broom (traditionally in the open doorway of a house). Ceremonies are usually held outside, in nature.

Shinto
Most weddings are held at Shinto shrines, usually in spring or autumn, but sometimes in a Buddhist temple or Christian church. The ceremony symbolizes the joining of two families as much as the joining of two individuals. Cups of sake are exchanged and twigs of the sacred sakaki tree are offered to the *kami* (spirit gods). Some devotees will not attend a marriage ceremony if they have recently been bereaved.

Zoroastrianism
The bride and groom (both dressed in white) sign a marriage contract. This is followed by a service during which married female relatives hold a white scarf over the couple's head. Two parts of the scarf are then sewn together to symbolize the couple's bond for the rest of their lives. Next, two crystallized sugar cones are ground together to represent a sweetening of the couple's life. The festivities that follow last between three and seven days.

Judaism

Weddings take place under a canopy known as a *chuppah* (sometimes constructed of a *talit,* or prayer shawl, stretched over four poles) to symbolize the home that the couple will build together and the presence of God over the marriage. At the end, the groom steps on and breaks a glass, as an expression of sorrow at the destruction of the Temple in Jerusalem – this gesture identifies the couple with the spiritual destiny of the Jewish people.

••• ✺ •••

TONGUE DIAGNOSIS: ACUPUNCTURE AND TIBETAN MEDICINE

Traditional Chinese Medicine (TCM) teaches that each area of the tongue relates to one or more different organs of the body (see right). Acupuncturists therefore examine the tongue to help with diagnosis: any abnormality in shape, colour or texture in a particular part of the tongue may point to a problem in the associated organ:

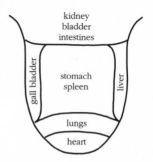

What to look for (TCM):

• A "normal" tongue is slightly moist, and is pale red or has a thin white coating.

• A thick white coating indicates that the patient has a cold.

• A sticky coating shows the presence of phlegm.

• Toothmarks down the middle of the tongue show a deficiency in spleen energy.

• A long, deep, midline crack that reaches to the tip may indicate weakness in the heart.

• A shallow crack that doesn't reach to the tip may show a deficiency in stomach energy (which can give rise to digestive problems).

Your tongue and your emotions (Tibet):

Tibetan physicians also diagnose states of mind from the tongue:

• If the tip of the tongue is very red, this can indicate repressed anger, jealousy or betrayal.

• A dark blue or blackish tinge on the left of the tongue could show deep obsessions or addictions.

• If the right-hand side of the tongue is pink with a flecked texture, this can indicate lying and unfaithfulness.

• A "muddy" tone at the back of the tongue can indicate psychological stress or imbalance.

• PSYCHOLOGICAL THEMES IN MYTH •

Some psychologists use myths as instruments of therapy. Their universal themes are validating and illuminating, and provide a counterweight to personal isolation. Myths can help people find meaning in their own lives, and come to terms with difficulties. Below are five key themes:

Abandoned children: Romulus and Remus (Rome) were abandoned and rescued by a wolf; Karna (Hinduism) was floated by his mother on a rush container on the River Acva (compare Moses).

Father–son rivalry: Cronus, the last-born Titan, castrated his divine father Uranos and was in turn overthrown by the Olympian god Zeus (Greece); Oedipus, discovering that he killed his father and married his mother as an oracle had foretold, blinded himself with his mother's brooch-pin (Greece).

Sibling rivalry: Seth and Horus fought for the throne of the gods, Horus having been conceived on the dead body of Osiris, whom his brother Seth had killed (Egypt).

Mortality and loss: Orpheus attempted to bring back his wife Eurydice from the Underworld after she had died of a snake bite, but lost her after disobeying an order not to look back at her (Greece).

Domestic violence: Philomela, princess of Athens, was raped by Tereus, husband of her sister Procne. He cut out her tongue so she could not speak of the crime, but she depicted it in a tapestry. In the end she and her sister were turned into birds by the gods (Rome).

• GHOSTS IN THE VIKING SAGAS •

Ghosts appear in the Viking Sagas as walking corpses, rather than faint disembodied spirits. There are two major types:

Haugbui: Mound-dwellers: dead bodies who lived on inside their tombs, and were never found far from them. Often treated their graves like homesteads, with mead-benches and roaring fires. Many had huge hoards of precious metals and treasures. Viciously attacked anyone who disturbed their mound or treasure.

Draugr: Also known as *aptrgangr* ("those who walk after death"). The wandering dead: animated corpses that roamed the countryside. They were huge and heavy, and could move through stone. Saga heroes often had to fight them in contests of strength. Some *draugr* could foretell the future, control the weather and even change shape. In the Sagas, they appear as seals, a flayed bull, an ear-less, tail-less, grey horse with a broken back, and a cat that would sit on a sleeper's chest and grow heavier, until the sleeper died of suffocation.

- 120 -

• • • A TYPICAL HINDU SHRINE • • •

Devout Hindu families worship (perform *puja*) at a home shrine as well as at the temple. It may be as simple as a small niche, appropriately furnished. There, prayers and mantras are chanted, flowers and fruits are offered to the god or goddess, and the deity's feet are bathed. A typical shrine will include:

• Images (*murti*) of a god, or gods – usually pictures or metal or stone statues
• Brass or silver pots for bathing the *murti*
• Colourful clothing to dress the *murti*
• A picture of the family's guru
• Flower garlands and a tray of fresh flowers (without stems), or petals
• An offering of freshly cooked food that has never been tasted during the course of its preparation (*prasad*)
• An incense burner and incense
• A small metal bell to invite the god or gods into the home, and to call the family together for prayer
• An oil lamp that remains lit throughout *puja*
• A lamp with a cotton string wick soaked in ghee (clarified butter) for waving light before the god or gods
• A camphor burner for passing fire before the god or gods
• Water cups and a small spoon for offering water to the god or gods
• Holy ash (*vibhuti*), sandalwood paste (*chandana*) and red powder (*kumkuma*) in metal containers, to mark worshippers' foreheads
• A metal tray to hold the *puja* implements, such as the bell and incense

••• ✿ •••

• • • THE STUPA TRADITION • • •

When the Buddha died, his remains were distributed in eight simple hemispherical burial mounds, created in India at places important in his life. In Sanskrit these mounds became known as *stupas* (literally "heaps").

More stupas were subsequently built all over South Asia (many by the 3rd-century Buddhist convert, Emperor Ashoka), each containing a sacred relic. These structures not only mark the Buddha's death but are a reminder of his life, teachings and enlightened mind. Stupas continue to be built today, and their design has become more elaborate. They are described as having five main parts, symbolizing the five elements and their relationship to the enlightened mind:

• square base: earth, equanimity
• hemispherical dome: water, indestructibility
• conical spire: fire, compassion
• crescent moon: wind, action
• circular disc, or jewel: space, awareness

+=══ ❋ ══=+

... *SANSKRIT ASANA NAMES* ...
DEMYSTIFIED

The Sanskrit names of many yoga poses sound complex and impenetrable at first encounter. However, each one is actually a basic description of the posture it represents – a combination of Sanskrit words for the animals, objects or deities that the pose resembles, parts of the anatomy used when doing it, or numbers or shapes relating to it. Below are explanations of seven key posture names. Note that each one ends with *asana*, simply meaning "pose".

SANSKRIT NAME	LITERAL TRANSLATION	ENGLISH NAME	REASON FOR NAME
Marjaryasana	*marjari*: cat *asana*: pose	Cat Pose	The rounding of the back, coupled with the arching of the back in a counterstretch, mimics the actions of a cat stretching
Adho mukha svanasana	*adho*: downward *mukha*: face *svana*: dog *asana*: pose	Downward-facing Dog Pose	Resembles a dog stretching
Urdva mukha svanasana	*urdva*: upward *mukha*: face *svana*: dog *asana*: pose	Upward-facing Dog Pose	Dogs (like yogis!) often do downward and upward stretches in succession as in this pose
Trikonasana	*tri*: three *kona*: angle *asana*: pose	Triangle Pose	The feet and upstretched hand form the three corners of a triangle
Tadasana	*tada*: mountain *asana*: pose	Mountain Pose	The body is strong, still and stable, like a mountain

Gomukhasana	*go*: cow *mukha*: face *asana*: pose	Cow-face Pose	The crossed legs are said to mimic the horns or lips of a cow, while the upward-pointing elbow resembles a cow's ear
Chaturanga dandasana	*chatur*: four *anga*: limb *danda*: staff *asana*: pose	Four-limbed Staff Pose	The body looks like a straight staff, supported by four small "limbs"

••• ✿ •••

••• THE SIX ARTICLES •••
 OF ISLAMIC BELIEF

According to a celebrated *hadith* (saying attributed to Mohammed), "Faith consists in affirming one's belief in Allah, His angels, His books, His messengers, the Last Day, and the divine destiny." These six articles are central to the Qur'anic concept of *iman* (faith):

Belief in God
Belief in Allah and His absolute sovereignty over the universe is the chief pillar of faith. The main purpose of existence is to worship God and bear witness to his name.

Belief in Angels
Angels figure prominently in the Qur'an. Believed to be winged beings of light who lack free will. The Angel Jibril (Gabriel) conveyed God's message to Mohammed.

Belief in the Sacred Texts
The Qur'an is literally the word of God. Other sacred texts, including the Torah and Christian gospels, are seen as divinely revealed, but the Qur'an, as the last revelation, has absolute authority.

Belief in Prophets
Islam accepts that there were thousands of prophets before Mohammed, but only 30 are mentioned by name in the Qur'an, among them Abraham, Isaac, Moses, Jacob, David, Solomon, Elisha and Jesus. Only some are accorded the higher status of *rasul* (messengers), chosen by God to advertise revelations of divine intent.

Belief in the Day of Judgment
A time when all creatures will undergo bodily resurrection and come face to face with divine justice. Those whose good deeds outweigh the evil they have done will go to heaven, the rest to hell.

Belief in Divinely Ordered Destiny
This is so closely entwined with "belief in God" that some Muslim scholars speak of only five articles of belief. The Qur'an states that all earthly events are recorded in advance, although individuals have responsibility for their own actions.

• • • *ZENER EXPERIMENTS* • • •

Karl Zener (1903–1964), Director of Psychological Studies at Duke University, North Carolina, developed Zener cards in the early 1930s as a tool to investigate ESP (extra-sensory perception). A pack consists of 25 cards in five designs: circle, cross, waves, square and circle. To create your own deck, copy the images below onto cards, making five of each design to create a set. Then try the following experiments with a partner:

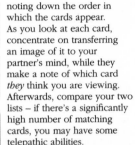

Test for clairvoyancy
(ability to read someone else's thoughts)
Shuffle the deck and ask your partner to slowly inspect the cards in turn, concentrating on each without letting you see it, and noting down the order. It helps to have a low screen between you. As each card is drawn, look at your partner and note down what *you* think he or she can see. Afterwards, compare notes – anyone with clairvoyant abilities should achieve an uncanny accuracy.

Test for telepathy
(ability to silently communicate thoughts to someone else's mind)
Shuffle the deck and slowly look at each card in turn, noting down the order in which the cards appear. As you look at each card, concentrate on transferring an image of it to your partner's mind, while they make a note of which card *they* think you are viewing. Afterwards, compare your two lists – if there's a significantly high number of matching cards, you may have some telepathic abilities.

Repeat these experiments a few times and then on several further occasions and compare the results. If you're consistently accurate, then there's a good chance that you genuinely have the skill you are being tested for.

• • • ❀ • • •

• *TEN LIFE-ENHANCING FOODS* •

Below are ten "super foods". Packed with all sorts of useful nutrients, these can help to protect your body from stress, prevent disease and improve overall health and vitality if included as part of your daily diet:

Leafy green vegetables
Phytochemicals in vegetables such as broccoli and spinach boost the immune and cardio-vascular systems, and protect bones and eyes. Broccoli, in particular, is rich in sulforaphane glucosinolate (SGS), which breaks down into sulforaphane, a powerful antioxidant that can even help to detoxify cancer-causing chemicals.

Squashes, carrots, sweet potato
Packed with valuable vitamins and minerals. High in fibre. Also rich in carotenoids – antioxidants

that balance the immune system, boost cell communication, deter cancer and heart disease, and lessen the risk of cataracts and other sight-related ailments.

Beans

Rich in vitamins. An excellent form of low-fat protein. They promote a healthy heart, help to regularize blood pressure, cholesterol and blood-sugar levels, and reduce the risk of diabetes.

Sprouted seeds

Possess high levels of antioxidants, which neutralize the free radicals responsible for much of the aging process and many degenerative diseases. Research has found that young broccoli sprouts have even more SGS (see *Leafy green vegetables*) than mature plants.

Nuts and seeds

Can help to reduce the risk of heart disease, diabetes, cancer and many other chronic diseases. Walnuts, for example, are rich in omega-3 fatty acids, plant sterols (important in lowering serum cholesterol), fibre, protein, vitamins, essential amino acids and minerals, and are high in antioxidants.

Berries

Blueberries, pomegranate and goji berries are all packed with antioxidants and therefore known for their anti-aging properties. All edible berries boost general health as well. Choose organic where possible, otherwise soak for an hour in cold water.

Oily fish

Fish such as salmon, trout, mackerel and fresh tuna are full of essential fatty acids, which increase "good" cholesterol, reduce high blood pressure and stabilize the heartbeat. Can alleviate arthritic conditions and improve eye health. Also, may help in treating depression, ADHD (attention deficit hyperactivity disorder), bipolar disorder and dementia.

Wheatgrass

Contains a wide range of vitamins, minerals and enzymes. Also an excellent source of amino acids, which help the body to produce proteins. It is a potent detoxifier, so should be introduced into a diet gradually.

Oats

High in protein, fibre, vitamins and minerals. Can help to reduce serum cholesterol levels and the risk of coronary heart disease. Can also have a beneficial effect on blood sugar levels and reduce the likelihood of diabetes.

Green tea

Drinking all types of tea can help to reduce gum disease and tooth decay, prevent kidney stones, and improve bone density. But green tea is particularly beneficial as it's less processed, and therefore higher in flavonoids (antioxidants that can reduce the risk of cancer, heart disease and stroke). It also contains less caffeine.

• THE PRINCIPAL AZTEC DEITIES •

Tezcatlipoca: "Lord of the Smoking Mirror" – which enabled him to prophesy and to look into people's hearts. The supreme god, associated with darkness, war and death.

Quetzalcoatl: "The Feathered Serpent". Part snake, part quetzal bird. Patron of priests, learning, crafts. Sailed away to sea on a raft: Hernan Cortés exploited the myth that he would one day return.

Tlaloc: God of rain, lightning, fertility. Children were sacrificed to him on mountaintops: if they cried, this was auspicious, for it suggested rain. Gave his name to the Aztec paradise, Tlalocan.

Chalchiuhtlicue: "Jade Skirt". Goddess of lakes and streams. The consort of Tlaloc, she had the power to cause hurricanes and floods.

Huitzilopochtli: "Hummingbird of the South". God of the sun and war, also known as Blue Tezcatlipoca. Also, the national god of the Aztecs. Focus of the Aztec cult of human sacrifice: human hearts were offered to him to keep the sun going round.

Xipe Totec: "The Flayed Lord". God of vegetation and springtime renewal. Sacrificial victims were flayed in his honour and their skins worn by the god's priests.

••• ❁ •••

• • • THE PAPAL PROPHECIES • • •

In 1595 Arnold de Wyon, a Benedictine historian, published a list of 112 Latin epithets – each condensing into a single phrase the reign of every pope from the time of Celestine II, elected in 1143, to the end of the world. De Wyon claimed that he had discovered the document in the papal archives and that it dated back to the 12th century, when it had been compiled by St Malachy, bishop of Armagh, Ireland (following a vision in which the entire future of the papacy was revealed to him).

Sceptics in modern times tend to be unsurprised that the "prophecies" referring to popes before the time of publicaton are accurate. Celestine II, for example, is characterized as *Ex Castro Tiberis* ("From a Castle on the Tiber"), and he was indeed born in the Umbrian town of Città di Castello, which stands on that river. However, post-1590 identifications are less clear-cut, and attempts to relate them to papal reigns often seem forced.

There have now been 111 popes from Celestine II, including the current pope, Benedict XVI, so the 112th prophecy would seem to refer to his successor. If so, prospects are bleak, for the final prediction reads:

> *"In a time of bitter persecution, the Holy See will be occupied by Petrus Romanus* ["Peter the Roman"], *who will feed his sheep through many tribulations: once these have come to an end, the city of the seven hills will be destroyed and the fearful judge will mete out judgment on his people. The End."*

... *KEY EVENTS IN THE* ...
LIFE OF THE BUDDHA

He was born c.566BCE to King Suddhodana and Queen Maya in the park of Lumbini (today part of Nepal), and named Siddharta Gautama. He is believed to have grown up in the nearby municipality of Kapilavastu, where he married his cousin, Yasodhara, at the age of 16.

Aged 29, he fathered a son, Rahula. Shortly after his son's birth, disillusioned by his life of luxury as a prince and troubled by the nature of life, death, sickness and suffering, he left his home and his family in search of a more fulfilling existence.

For six years, he lived a harsh, ascetic life as a mendicant in the Ganges valley, travelling with his five disciples, teaching and meditating.

Aged 35, near starvation, he accepted food from a young woman to regain his strength, causing his disciples to leave him in disgust. Alone, he sat under the bodhi tree in Bodh Gaya, meditating until he had achieved enlightenment. From this time on he was known as the Buddha (meaning "the awakened one" in Sanskrit).

Seven weeks after his enlightenment, he left Bodh Gaya and travelled to Sarnath, where he delivered the first sermon of his teachings (*dharma*) in a deer park (*see p71*) to the five disciples who had earlier abandoned him. These five became the basis of the *sangha* (the Buddhist community of monks and nuns).

For the following 45 years the Buddha dedicated himself to teaching the truths he had realized. During this time he performed a number of "miracles": in one instance he used *metta* (loving kindness) to calm a mad elephant, which his jealous cousin Devadatta had set upon him.

In 485BCE, aged 80, he ate his final meal – of pork, given to him by a blacksmith called Cunsa, which may well have been the cause of his death. He is recorded to have lain down on his right side, between two shala trees near the town of Kushinagara, and meditated before passing away. On his death he achieved final nirvana (*parinirvana*).

• • • 108 AS A HOLY NUMBER • • •

• 108 is a three-digit multiple of 3, whose numbers add up to 9 – 3 times 3.*

• Mathematically, 108 is an "abundant", or "excessive", number: this means that all its divisors (numbers that divide into it, except the number itself) add up to more than 108.

• 108 is also a "semi-perfect" number: a selection of its divisors can be added up to make 108.

• Hindus and Buddhists use *malas* – circular strings of 108 beads to count their mantra repetitions when chanting. The beads are held in the right hand and moved through the fingers, as with a Catholic rosary. A larger, 109th bead marks the end of each cycle.

• Sikhs also use *malas* in prayer. The device is made up of 108 knots tied along a string of wool.

• According to yogic tradition, there are 108 holy sites (*pithas*) in India.

• Each Hindu deity has 108 names.

• Lord Krishna had 108 *gopis*, or maidservants.

• Nataraj, the cosmic-dancing form of the Hindu god Shiva, moves through 108 poses.

• Traditional Indian classical dance, or *Bharatanatyam*, has 108 key poses and transitions (called *karanas*).

• Wu-style *tai chi chuan*, a form of tai chi, has 108 movements.

• Buddhism teaches that there are 108 mortal desires. Thus, Buddhist temples often have 108 steps. And it's a Japanese Buddhist New Year tradition to chime a temple bell 108 times, each ring representing the destruction of one mortal temptation.

* The number 3 represents eternal balance: birth, life and death; body, mind and spirit; the Christian Holy Trinity; and the three primary aspects of the Divine in Hinduism – Brahma the creator, Vishnu the preserver and Shiva the destroyer.

••• ✿ •••

• • • SIX BUDDHIST FESTIVALS • • •

Buddhist New Year: Held in April in parts of SE Asia and Sri Lanka; but at different times elsewhere. The Tibetan New Year, called Losar, is in January or February. Here the festival has a monastic flavour. Generally, the New Year is a time of rejoicing and hope, with fireworks and feasting.

Vesak *("Buddha Day"):* Held in April or, in India, the first full moon in May. Often known as "Buddha's birthday", though in fact it celebrates his birth, life and passing (*paranirvana*). Vesak is the name of the month in the Indian calendar.

Dharma Day: Held at the full moon in July. Celebrates the Buddha's teachings, remembering that after he became enlightened, he immediately shared his experience with his first five disciples. Readings and meditations are performed. A time for reflection, and for gratitude to teachers.

Ulambana *(Ancestor Day):*
Held in August. The gates of Hell
are thought to open on the first
day of this Mahayana festival.
Spirits may visit our world for
the next 15 days, and food
offerings are made to relieve their
sufferings. On the fifteenth day
(Ulambana itself) offerings are
made to ancestors at cemeteries.

Sangha Day: Held at the full
moon in March (more strictly,
the Indian month of Magha).
Commemorates the "fourfold
assembly" – when 1,250 disciples
converged from their wanderings,
meeting spontaneously in a
monastery to pay respect to the
Buddha.

Paranirvana Day: Held at
the full moon in February.
Commemorates the Buddha's
death, in the awareness that
death is not to be regretted
in an impermanent world. An
occasion to think about mortality.
Meditations are performed to
support the deceased.

••• ✷ •••

• HOW TO GIVE SPIRITUAL HEALING •

Many of us have the power to heal without being aware of the fact.
The underlying principles are mysterious. Explanations range from bio-
magnetic energy to divine intervention. Try the following exercise on a
volunteer to explore your own healing potential:

1. Rub your hands together
vigorously. Then hold them a
few inches apart and facing each
other, as if holding a ball. Slowly
and gently "bounce" your hands
in and out. Feel the energy change
as your hands move closer to, and
further away, from each other.

2. Imagine that in the centre of
one palm is a circular patch that
can transmit energy. Rub here
with the thumb of your other
hand, visualizing that you are
"opening up" this area. If you
have any spiritual beliefs, call on
them for help in your healing.
Repeat with the other hand.

3. Ask your subject to sit in a
comfortable chair, relax, close his
or her eyes and breathe naturally.

4. Stand near your patient, with
your feet shoulder-width apart.

Breathe deeply and imagine
your heart chakra (in the chest)
pulsing with energy. Feel the
crown chakra (at the top of
your head) opening up to allow
healing energy in. Visualize this
energy flowing down into your
heart, along your arms and into
your hands.

5. Direct this energy to where
you feel it is needed. If you're
unsure, hold your hands near
your subject's major chakra sites
(*see p24*) – to try to get more of a
sense of their energy imbalances.

6. If you find, as you work,
that your hands become stiff
or uncomfortable, firmly shake
them (as if flicking off water) to
release any negative energy you
may have picked up. Take time
throughout to stop, breathe deeply
and connect to the healing energy.

THE LEGEND OF THE ORIGINS OF VASTU

Vastu shastra is the Indian feng shui – the art of placement. Like feng shui, it has a template that can be superimposed over any building. However, unlike the feng shui pa kua (*see p36*), the *vastu* template has a humanoid shape – the Purusha (shown below).

According to legend, a creature created by the Hindu god Brahma grew into a giant, all-devouring demon. Fellow gods Shiva and Vishnu told Brahma of their fear that this giant would consume them all, so Brahma called upon the gods of the eight cardinal directions, who crept up on the demon and pinned him to the earth. But this was not enough to hold him down: it took 45 gods in the end, including Brahma.

The demon complained that he was being punished unfairly – after all, he was only following the nature that Brahma had given him. A compromise was reached: the creature – who was newly named Vastu Purusha – would become immortal on the condition that he never again left his current position on the Earth. In return, anyone wanting to build a new house or other structure must first pay reverence to him. If you conformed with this, you would be blessed; otherwise, you would risk the demon's wrath. The *vastu* grid below shows the positions of the 45 gods on the demon – including Brahma, who sits in the centre, on Vastu Purusha's navel:

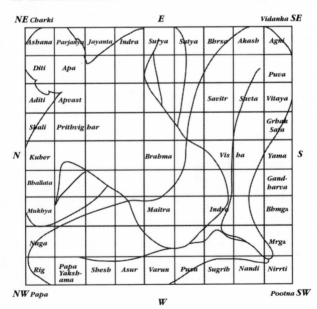

... TAROT: THE ...
MAJOR ARCANA

The Tarot is divided into the Major and Minor Arcana. The Major Arcana comprise 22 of the 78 cards in the deck, and form the imaginative and spiritual core of the Tarot. They deal in universal themes, mainly via archetypes, whether through personifications, such as Judgment and Strength, or through characters, such as the Fool and the Hanged Man. (The 56 cards of the Minor Arcana are organized into four suits: Wands, Cups, Swords and Pentacles.)

Each symbol is depicted within a setting, which itself has symbolic meanings – for example, the Fool is walking off a precipice, which may indicate recklessness, or perhaps a leap of faith. In many decks each card also has a name and a number – though not all decks have both (the absence of names on the earliest decks may be explained by the fact that many using the Tarot would have been illiterate).

Below are the traditional associations – a starting point for Tarot readings, with the caveat that the rich symbolism of the cards cannot be reduced to a simplistically coded interpretation. (*See also p27*.)

ARCANA CARD	NUMBER	INTERPRETATION
The Fool	0	The quest for enlightenment, Everyman
The Magician	I	Skill, creativity, transformation
The High Priestess	II	Moral law, insight, mystery
The Empress	III	Comfort, fertility, desire
The Emperor	IV	Action, leadership, virility
The Hierophant	V	Enlightenment, spiritual energy, institution
The Lovers	VI	Union, love and passion
The Chariot	VII	Victory, self-conviction, discipline
Strength	VIII or XI	Confidence, courage, inner power
The Hermit	IX	Introspection, self-sufficiency, solitude
The Wheel of Fortune	X	Major change, precarious balance, possibility
Justice	XI or VIII	Balance, duality, impartiality
The Hanged Man	XII	Realignment, sacrifice, patience
Death	XIII	Transition, profound change, loss
Temperance	XIV	Self-control, harmony, synthesis
The Devil	XV	Trial, self-examination, sexuality
The Tower	XVI	Chaos, transformation, revelation
The Star	XVII	Hope, replenishment, serenity
The Moon	XVIII	Illusion, imagination, doubt
The Sun	XVIII	Joy, enthusiasm, innocence
Judgment	XX	Divine judgment, transformation
The World	XXI	Completion, unity

• • • TEN HEALING CRYSTALS • • •

To benefit from the therapeutic qualities of the following crystals, carry the appropriate one with you or place it in your home or workplace.

CRYSTAL	EMOTIONAL BENEFITS	PHYSICAL COMPLAINTS TREATED
Amethyst	Purifies, calms anger, brings control, breaks old patterns	Blood impurities, insomnia, headaches, arthritis, any general pain
Bloodstone	Gives courage and balance, calms agitation	Painful menstruation, nosebleeds, hip and joint problems
Carnelian	Gives courage, motivates, heals jealousy, promotes self-confidence	Thyroid problems, infections, poor digestion, anorexia
Citrine	Promotes fun, creativity and clear self-expression, helps decision-making	Toxicity, nervous system ailments, allergies
Crystal (quartz)	Awakens the soul to higher levels of awareness, repels negativity, brings stability	Heart complaints, bad backs, ear problems, nausea, general aches and pains
Jade	Soothes, balances, promotes flexibility and tolerance	Asthma, eye, heart muscle, bone, kidney and bladder problems
Peridot	Clears stuck or repressed emotions, lessens jealousy	Depression, mental problems; liver, spleen, pancreas, intestine, bowel and gall bladder issues
Tiger's Eye	Develops insight, gives a sense of grounding, calms an overactive imagination, focuses the mind	Over-indulgence, headaches, indigestion, skin disease
Tourmaline	Helps in self-forgiveness and mending a broken heart, calms the soul	Lymphatic and digestive system issues, swelling
Turquoise	Gives strength and courage, boosts fulfilment and success, helps in public speaking	Lung conditions, rheumatism, arthritis, sore throat

••• ✦ •••

• ANGEL MISCELLANY •

• The earliest representation of an angel is on a limestone stele found in the Sumerian temple of E-Nun-makh, in the city formerly known as Ur. It shows the king Ur-Nammu at prayer with an angel, who is pouring water from a vase. Dates from c.2300BCE.

• Based on human dimensions, an angel weighing 150lb (just under 70kg) would need wings about 6 or 7ft (2m) long to enable flight. The being would also need immense pectoral muscles – at least 15 per cent of the total body weight (human pectorals are only about 5 per cent of body weight). This suggests that angels cannot, physiologically, be human beings with wings, as so frequently depicted in art.

• Jews, Christians and Zoroastrians all share the belief that every human being has a guardian angel watching over him or her. Muslims believe that each person has four angels, or *malaa'ika* – two recording their good deeds, the other two their bad.

• A 2008 survey, by Baylor's Institute for Studies of Religion, found that 55 per cent of Americans claim to have been "protected from harm by a guardian angel".

• According to St Thomas Aquinas, angels are pure spirit: they have no mass or body, and because they do not move in worldly time, they can exert their powers successively in places far apart. Such ideas have been used to support the theory of Matthew Fox and Rupert Sheldrake (in *The Physics of Angels*) that angels could, in fact, be photons.

••• ✿ •••

• • • NINE FLOWER REMEDIES • • •
FOR MODERN PROBLEMS

Dr Edward Bach (1886–1936) developed 38 flower essences, using English flowering plants, in the 1930s. The principle has been extended in the last 30 years to cover modern problems using plants from all over the world, including Australia, the Himalayas and the Amazon. Recent pioneers include Ian White (Australian Bush Essences), Richard Katz (Flower Essence Society) and Judy Griffin (Petite Fleur Texan range).

Almond Blossom Essence: Among other things, good for teenage mood swings

Aloe Vera Essence: Recommended for workaholics and people who suffer from exhaustion and burnout

Boab Essence: Used to treat genetic ailments that arise in emotional patterns passed down through the family. Freedom from the past

Cherry Blossom Essence: Promotes lightheartedness, esp. in children with separated parents

Electro Essence (Australian Bush Essences): Counteracts negative effects of cell phones and computers

Lotus Essence: Promotes clarity, awareness, whole self harmony. Good for meditation and creative visualization

Orchid Queen Essence: Helps to heal the female psyche, instilling the wonder and joy of womanhood

Red Suva Frangipani Essence: Restores calm after emotional turmoil or relationship break-up

Wedding Bush Essence: Empowers those who find commitment difficult, to a person or to a goal

✦━✶━✦

• • • *FIVE USEFUL MUDRAS* • • •

The Sanskrit word *mudra* means "seal" or "sign". In yoga, mudras
are positions of the hands and fingers used in meditation to "seal"
energy (*prana*) into the body, or to send it in a particular direction.
Mudras are also important in Buddhism. Different mudras are said to
elicit different responses in body and mind. They can also be used
ideogrammatically, to transmit symbolic meanings.

Anjali, or Namaste, Mudra
The traditional greeting in Hinduism – it resembles
the common Christian prayer position. Bring your
hands together in front of you, fingers straight
upward; your thumbs may touch your sternum. The
mudra harmonizes right and left sides of the brain
and nourishes the heart chakra. *Namaste* means "I
bow to the divinity within you from the divinity within me."

Dhyani Mudra
Useful to help with concentration during
meditation – the light tension between the thumbs
helps focus the mind. Rest the back of your right
hand in your left palm, thumbs gently touching.
The upper hand symbolizes the state of enlightenment; the
lower hand, the illusory world, or *samsara*. Hence, the mudra
symbolizes the victory of enlightenment over *samsara*, and the
ultimate unity of these states.

Chin, or Jnana, Mudra ("seal of knowledge")
A classic meditation position. Bring your thumbs and index fingers
together, the nails of your index fingers touching pads of your thumbs.
Relax your other fingers. The circle formed between each index finger
and thumb represents the merging of the individual
with the universal soul. This mudra directs the flow of
prana to the upper chakras, aiding concentration.

Kapitthaka, or Smiling Buddha, Mudra
A gesture of happiness that opens the flow of energy to the
heart. Bend your ring and little fingers, pressing them down
with the thumb, keeping index and middle fingers straight
but relaxed. Concentrate on your third eye or brow chakra
(*see p24*).

Lotus Mudra
A gesture of purity. Place your palms together
and spread your fingers, keeping the base of your
hands, your thumbs and your little fingers together,
so that your hands look like open lotus petals.
Use during times of isolation or despair to
lift your spirits.

• • • VISIONS OF ATLANTIS • • •

The first mention of the legendary island of Atlantis is found in two dialogues by Plato, written c.360BCE. He describes how the island grew as a naval power some 9,000 years before the time of Solomon until, after a failed attempt to conquer Athens, it sank into the sea "in a single day and night of misfortune". More than a millennium and a half later, in the early 17th century, Francis Bacon used Atlantis as the geographic model for a utopian society off the coast of America. Later still the notion caught the imagination of the American psychic Edgar Cayce, who in 1923 described how Atlantis had been an advanced civilization, whose refugees had emigrated to ancient Egypt, Morocco and pre-Columbian America. The Atlanteans had electricity, as well as ships and planes driven by crystal power – indeed, it was overcharging of crystal that caused the demise of the civilization in a massive explosion.

••• ❀ •••

• • • POPULAR CHINESE HERBS • • •

In Chinese herbalism each medicinal plant used is classified according to its essence, its action, its direction and its contracting or dispersing effects. Ginseng, for example, is classified as warm, tonifying, moistening, ascending and contracting. A traditional Chinese herbalist will mix herbs expertly to suit the patient, adding further ingredients to balance yin/yang and others to counter toxicity or side-effects. Below are four of the most popular Chinese herbs that exhibit such striking medical properties that they could justly be claimed as "superfoods".

Shiitake mushroom
Contains compounds that lower blood cholesterol levels and block the effects of highly saturated fats. Also contains lentinan, which stimulates the immune system to produce interferon, helpful in fighting viruses and cancer.

Black tree mushroom
Also called the mo-er mushroom, or sometimes the tree ear or wood ear mushroom. Used as a tonic to promote longevity and to help with painful menstruation. In addition, contains adenosine and other blood-thinning compounds that help to provide protection against strokes and heart attacks.

Dang-gui (Angelica sinensis)
Used to harmonize qi energy, increase coronary circulation and reduce blood pressure. Also has anti-flammatory, pain-reducing and tranquillizing effects on the cerebral nerves, and is used in treating irregular menstruation and PMS and in helping recovery from childbirth.

Ginkgo (Ginkgo biloba)
Used to treat pulmonary and heart diseases and to regulate urine emission. It expands the blood vessels, improves circulation, and prevents blood from clotting. Ginkgo extracts are widely used in the West to help brain function and treat depression.

... *UNPLEASANT DREAMS* ...
AND WHAT THEY MEAN

Dreams are not squeamish, nor do they obey social niceties. Their content can seem crude to the waking mind. But if bodily functions frequently appear in dreams, that's because the body offers a universal repertoire of powerful symbolism. Here are some possible meanings of uncomfortable dream situations that are commonly experienced:

Urinating/ defecating in public: Very common. Urinating may represent spontaneous self-expression, while defecation symbolizes creativity. One interpretation is that the dreamer has yet to find a way of expressing his or her true self.

Being naked in public: May indicate a fear of self-revelation, whether for social reasons (such as class anxiety) or because the dreamer feels inferior intellectually or emotionally, or simply uninteresting.

Being chased: Often, whatever or whoever is chasing the dreamer represents an aspect of themselves that seeks to make contact with them. Being chased by an animal may suggest that one's instinctual nature longs to be expressed (suggesting a lifestyle that is too cerebral or repressed).

Being unprepared: A dream of failing to prepare for an exam, for speaking in public, or for running a race, may symbolize all kinds of anxieties, including fears of professional or emotional inadequacy. Such dreams are often experienced by perfectionists.

Being attacked: An attack or threat by an unpleasant, violent, angry or overly sexual person usually represents the "Shadow" archetype (*see p114*) – the part of our psyche we try to hide from ourselves.

••• ✿ •••

• *HOW TO REMEMBER NUMBERS* •

Committing things to memory, rather than writing them down, helps to keep your brain in trim, even into old age. Use one of these methods to remember phone numbers, personal identity numbers or dates:

Number rhyme system:
Translate each digit into a rhyme word, and create memorable pictures or a surreal narrative using the images they conjure up:

0 Hero *1* Sun *2* Shoe *3* Tree *4* Door *5* Hive *6* Sticks *7* Heaven
8 Gate *9* Wine *10* Hen

Number shape system:
Translate each digit into a similar shape; then proceed as above:

0 Baseball *1* Pencil *2* Swan *3* Handcuffs *4* Sailboat *5* Snake or
Hook *6* Elephant's trunk *7* Streetlight *8* Snowman *9* Balloon on a
string *10* Knife and plate

• • • THE 72 NAMES OF GOD • • •

The *Zohar*, a 2,000-year-old commentary on the Hebrew Bible and the Torah, is the most important text in the Kabbalist tradition. In it, we learn that Moses revealed the 72 names of God (encoded) in the Book of Exodus (14: 19–21). Each Hebrew letter in the names is said to function as a spiritual power in its own right. The secret names give us control over chaos – symbolized by the parting of the Red Sea. Some Kabbalists say that scanning over the names (right to left) helps to raise our spiritual consciousness, even if we do not know how to pronounce them:

כהת	אכא	ללה	מהש	עלם	סיט	ילי	והו
הקם	הרי	מבה	יול	ההע	לאו	אלד	הוי
וזהו	מלה	ייי	ולך	פהל	לוו	כלי	לאו
ועיר	לכב	אום	רוי	עיאה	ידת	האא	נתה
ייי	רהע	וועם	אני	מנד	כוק	להו	יזו
מיה	עשל	ערי	סאל	ילה	וול	מיכ	ההה
פוי	מבה	נית	גוא	עמם	הוזש	רוי	והו
מווי	עוו	ידד	ונב	מצר	הדרו	ייל	נמם
מום	היי	יבמ	ראה	וזבי	איע	מונק	רמב

••• ✿ •••

• • YOUR PERSONAL YEAR NUMBER • •

Numerology is the art of reading one's destiny by the study of numbers. Often, numerologists start by working out their subject's Personal Year Number, which determines the underlying theme of a particular calendar year for that individual. To calculate this, take your month and day of birth and the year in question, and add their component numbers together. For example, if you were born on April 19 and the year is 2010, you'd add $(0 + 4) + (1 + 9) + (2 + 0 + 1 + 0) = 4 + 10 + 3 = 17 = 1 + 7 = 8$ (your Personal Year Number). Here are the main influences for the numbers 1–9: 1 = Opportunities, 2 = Balance, 3 = Creativity, 4 = Building Foundations, 5 = Communication, 6 = Commitments, 7 = Materialization, 8 = Rebirth, 9 = Endings and Beginnings. Knowing that your theme for the year is rebirth will help you understand the significance of events as they unfold for you, and will help you with your decision-making.

• • • HOME BACK CLASS • • •

Osteopaths and chiropractors are good at easing the sufferings of people with back and neck problems, often avoiding the need for drugs or surgery. It's advisable to consult a qualified practitioner for advice on any problems related to your back or neck. However, practitioners often recommend a DIY routine like the one below to ease pain and stiffness, and to keep the spine supple:

1. Lie on your back on the floor. Bring your knees up to your chest and clasp your hands under them. Keeping your whole body as relaxed as possible, pull your knees in toward your chest slowly. Hold for 10 seconds, then release. Repeat several times.

2. Get onto all fours with your hands directly under your shoulders and your knees directly under your hips. Gently round your back as if you were an angry cat, letting your head drop and your pelvis tuck in. Hold for about 20 seconds, then release. Repeat several times.

3. Sit on the edge of a chair with your feet firmly on the floor, quite wide apart. Slowly bend forward, hands reaching toward the floor, head moving between your knees. Feel a gentle stretch (stop if it hurts). Hold for about 20 seconds, then gently return to the starting position.

• FIVE TYPES OF MEDITATION •

Meditation is the art of stilling the mind. The best way to start is to sit quietly, back straight, eyes closed, breathing easily. Notice each thought as it arises. The idea is to remain detached from your thoughts and avoid reacting: just let them go. Allow them to drift out of your mind, just as they drifted in. Do this for 5–10 minutes. The benefits are subtle but significant. Progress when you feel ready to one of the following meditation types.

Breathing: Concentrate on each in-breath, each out-breath and each pause in between. If your attention wanders, gently bring it back and continue.

Candle: Gently focus your eyes on a candle flame as it flickers. Maintain this soft gaze.

Counting: Slowly count from 1 to 20 in your head, keeping your full attention on each number. If you get distracted, go back to 1 and start again.

Sound: Choose a sacred sound or mantra (*Om* is a favourite: *see p18*). Quietly and slowly repeat the sound, keeping your full attention on it. Be mindful of what you're saying – the meaning as well as the sound.

Mandala: Focus on a mandala – a sacred diagram (*see p110*). Inhabit its ineffable centre, the mystery at the heart of being. Let the design sit in your mind, and your mind dwell on the design. Lose and find yourself.

・ ・ ・ BALANCING ENERGIES: ・ ・ ・
ALTERNATE NOSTRIL BREATHING

The *ida* and *pingala nadis* are our main yogic energy channels, spiralling up around our spine. *Ida nadi* starts on the left side of the *sushumna* (central channel) and winds its way up to the left nostril; the *pingala* starts on the right and winds in the opposite direction up to the right nostril *(see p104)*. *Ida nadi* is responsible for "female" energy, corresponding with the cool, calm power of the moon and with restorative rest. *Pingala nadi* controls "male" energy, associated with the hot, strong energy of the sun and with alertness. An imbalance in these energies can lead to our feeling either slow and sluggish, or overly active and ambitious. Alternate nostril breathing, or *nadi shodana*, helps to balance the opposing energies within each of us. No other exercise purifies the *nadis* quite so rapidly or thoroughly. It is good to perform at least ten rounds of this technique before you start meditating.

1. Gently curl your right index and middle fingers in toward your right palm to create the *Vishnu mudra*.

2. Place your thumb lightly on your right nostril and your ring and little fingers lightly on your left nostril. Exhale through both nostrils.

3. Use your thumb to close your right nostril, and inhale slowly and steadily through your left nostril for 2 seconds.

4. Hold your breath for 8 seconds, closing your left nostril using your ring and little fingers. Relax your thumb to open your right nostril and exhale fully for 4 seconds.

5. In the same way, inhale through your right nostril, close it, then open your left nostril and exhale through it. This is one round. Practice five or ten rounds to start feeling more balanced. The proportions of breaths should always be 1:4:2.

・・・❁・・・

HOW TO MAKE HERBAL COUGH DROPS

1. Put 1 cup (50g) horehound dried leaves and 1 tablespoon (15ml) Balm of Gilead into a saucepan.
2. Add 2 cups (500ml) water and simmer for about 20 minutes.
3. Strain into a pan, add 2 cups (400g) unrefined sugar and, if desired for flavour, a couple of drops of lemon essential oil or lemon extract.
4. Boil rapidly until the mixture reaches 230°F (110°C) on a candy thermometer and you can "spin a thread".
5. Scoop up a teaspoon of the mixture and scrape it off with another spoon to release it into a bowl of cold water.
6. With a slotted spoon, remove this "drop" from the water after just a second or two – before it gets too hard.
7. Drain it and roll in powdered sugar, which will stop the drops from sticking together. Repeat steps 5–7 until you've used all your mixture.

+=※=+

• • • *OGHAM* • • •

The Celtic Ogham is an early medieval alphabet, made up of twenty characters all easily drawn with simple upward and downward strokes. It was originally used in Ireland and Britain. Most surviving inscriptions are names, created by groups of characters. However, each individual character is also thought to have its own potent symbolism, including a particular human quality and a sacred tree.

LETTER	NAME	SACRED TREE	SYMBOL	MEANING
B	Beith (pron. BEH)	Birch		Beginning, renewal, cleansing
L	Luis (pron. LWEESH)	Rowan		Protection, connection, control of senses
F	Fern (pron. FAIRN)	Alder		Strength, passion, prophecy
S	Sail (pron. SEHL)	Willow		Intuition, vision
N	Nion (pron. NEE-on)	Ash		Connection, wisdom
H	Uath (pron. OO-ah)	Hawthorn		Relationships, consequence, protection
D	Dair (pron. DAH-r)	Oak		Strength, stability, protection
T	Tinne (pron. CHIN-yuh)	Holly		Action, objectivity
C	Coll (pron. CULL)	Hazel		Creativity, honesty
Q	Ceirt (pron. KAIRT)	Apple		Beauty, love

M	Muin (pron. MUHN)	Vine		Introspection, relaxation, prophecy
G	Gort (pron. GORT)	Ivy		Determination, change, search for self
NG	nGéadal (pron. NYEH-al)	Reed		Harmony, growth, direct action
STR	Straif (pron. STRAHF)	Blackthorn		Discipline, control, cleansing
R	Ruis (pron. RWEESH)	Elder		Transition, evolution
A	Ailm (pron. AHL-m)	Silver Fir		Clarity, energy, clear-sightedness
O	Onn (pron. UHN)	Gorse or Furze		Resourcefulness, transmutation
U	Úr (pron. OOR)	Heather		Dreams, romance, healing
E	Eadhadh (pron. EH-wah)	Aspen or Poplar		Transformation, vision, rebirth
I	Iodhadh (pron. EE-wah)	Yew		Passage, rebirth, illusion

••• 💮 •••

••• ORTHODOX EASTER •••

In Orthodox Christianity, Easter is determined by the date of Passover
– because the Last Supper shared by Jesus and his disciples was a *seder*
(the ritual meal eaten at Passover). During Easter, believers sing: "Christ
is risen from the dead, trampling down death by death, and upon those
in the tombs bestowing life." From Easter to Pentecost, they greet each
other with "Christ is risen!" The response is, "Indeed He is risen!"

• • • *FRUITY HOME BEAUTY* • • •

Organic fruits can be used as a basis for home beauty treatments that are not only highly effective but also completely natural – unlike most standard cosmetic preparations these days, which are packed with chemicals. Note that facepacks, such as those suggested with avocado and banana, should be used no more than once a week. If you have sensitive skin, try a small patch test behind your ear first.

Apple: To stave off dandruff, massage apple juice into the scalp and leave for about 15 minutes before rinsing.

Avocado: To nourish dry and mature skin, blend 2 teaspoons of avocado flesh with 1 teaspoon of yoghurt and 1 teaspoon of runny honey; apply, leave for 15 minutes, and then rinse off with warm water. The rough side of the avocado skin can also be used to rub away dead skin on elbows and heels.

Banana: To revitalize dry skin, mix 1 tablespoon (15ml) of mashed banana with 1 teaspoon of runny honey; apply, leave for 15–20 minutes, then rinse with warm water. To condition dry, frizzy hair, make a smooth paste from some mashed banana and grapeseed oil (about half a cup of the paste should be enough); apply, leave for at least an hour, then wash your hair with shampoo, as normal.

Lemon: To make a good toner for oily skin as well as an effective rinse for greasy hair, dilute 1 tablespoon (15ml) lemon juice with 2 cups (500ml) distilled water.

Papaya: To treat pimples or acne, mix 2 teaspoons of mashed papaya with 1 teaspoon of plain yoghurt, and apply to the affected areas; leave for 10–15 minutes, then rinse with warm water. To reduce puffiness around the eyes, place thin slices of papaya over closed eyelids.

Pineapple: To make a softener for nail cuticles, blend 2 tablespoons (30ml) of pineapple juice with 2 teaspoons of cider vinegar. Soak your nails in this mixture for 20–30 minutes. Then rinse and dry.

+━ ✳ ━+

• • • SIX FEMALE MONSTERS • • •
IN SOUTH AMERICAN MYTH

Female monsters and evil shape-shifters stalk through South American mythology and folklore. Here are six of those most feared:

La Tunda *(Colombia):* Appears to victims as a loved one, luring them into the forest. Here she keeps them in a trance by feeding them shrimps on which she has passed wind; identifiable by wooden leg in shape of a kitchen utensil.

La Patasola *(Colombia):* "One Foot." Beautiful, often familiar-looking woman who reveals her true monstrous one-legged form after a time, sucking her victims' blood or devouring their flesh.

La Sayona *(Venezuela):* The spirit of a woman who appears only to adulterous men, luring them away and devouring them.

La Llorona or the Weeping Woman *(Guatemala, Chile, Mexico):* A spirit who is always crying, usually for her children whom she has drowned. Her appearance often presages death.

La Mojana or Mami Wata *(Amazon basin):* A shape-shifting water demon who appears in human form to seduce and take away luckless humans.

La Candileja *(Colombia):* The spirit of a vicious old woman whose grandchildren grew up to be murderers and thieves. Damned to travel the world in a ring of flames.

• • • ❁ • • •

• • • GEOPATHIC STRESS • • •

The earth has a natural magnetic field, created by electrical currents in the molten metals within its core. It radiates energies that at normal levels have little or no impact on our daily lives. However, features such as geological fault lines and subsoil cavities (tunnels, mines, underground streams) can distort them, causing the radiation to be harmful – causing effects known collectively as geopathic stress (GS). Experts believe that GS can cause insomnia, migraines, depression, ME and even cancer, among other illnesses. Certain countries, including Germany and Austria, actually legislate against building houses over GS zones for this reason.

GS emerges in thin lines and can therefore pass through just one chair or side of the bed. Watch out for tell-tale signs. Cats love GS and often sleep on a bad spot, whereas dogs avoid it at all costs, and babies will roll to one corner of their cot to keep away from it. If you suspect you have a problem, put cork tiles under your bed or favourite chair for a week and see if you feel any better. However, bear in mind that the tiles will neutralize the rays only for a limited period. Switching on a hairdryer and running the side of it over your clothed body is also said to counter the effects. If you suspect you have a serious problem, contact a GS surveyor who will use dowsing techniques to assess the levels and location of radiation in your home.

Human touch can be highly therapeutic, and giving a home massage is a particularly effective way to soothe aching muscles and boost someone's feeling of well-being, as well as showing love, trust and affection to the person concerned.

Choose a room that is private and warm, and set aside adequate space for your subject to lie down – perhaps on a sturdy table, well-padded with towels, otherwise, on padding on the floor. Warm your massage oil by placing it in a bowl on a radiator. Sweet almond oil is ideal. If you wish, add a couple of drops of an essential oil (*see p148 for their various properties*) to enhance the experience with aromatherapy. Don't worry too much about technique. Just keep asking whether the pressure is right and if everything feels comfortable. However, here are some basic massage strokes to help get you started:

Effleurage: With the palms and fingers of both hands, lightly stroke upward and back again in a continuous sweeping motion. Good on any part of the body, at the start and end of a massage, and as a linking movement in the transfer between different areas.

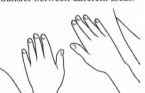

Rolling: Gather the flesh between the fingers and thumb of both hands and compress it gently before rolling back down. Best on soft tissue areas of the body and toward the end of a massage in order to enliven the skin.

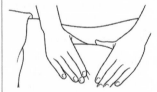

Hacking: Make gentle karate chops with alternate hands (moving them from the wrists and not the elbows). Strike the skin frequently, and with only the tips of your fingers. Best on fleshier areas of the body and in the middle of a massage.

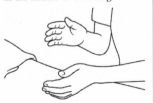

Cupping: Make loose cup shapes with your hands and, with the palms facing downward, flick your wrists alternately to strike the skin lightly, making a hollow sound. Best on fleshier areas of the body and toward the end of a massage.

• *THE ELEUSINIAN MYSTERIES* •

Every year in Eleusis in ancient Greece secret initiation rituals were performed in honour of the corn goddess Demeter and her daughter Persephone. The initiates were offered union with the divine, god-like powers and rewards in the afterlife. In a great hall called the Telesterion, celebrants gazed on the sacred relics of Demeter. What happened next is an enigma, for no one was permitted to say, on pain of death. Some experts believe the climax was a drug-fuelled night of dancing, followed by a bull sacrifice.

••• ✿ •••

• • *THE FIVE DAILY DUTIES AND* • •
FIVE CONSTANT DUTIES OF HINDUISM

Every devout Hindu is meant to perform *pancha maha vagnas* (the five daily duties) and *pancha nitya karmas* (the five constant duties) in their everyday life to ensure spiritual prosperity:

The Five Daily Duties

1. *Deva yagna:* Worship the family god at the home shrine (*see p121*). This is known as *puja*, and might involve chanting, prayer, meditation, scripture study, and/or bathing and dressing an image of the deity.

2. *Brahma yagna:* Study the Vedas and other scriptures to refresh the mind with sacred knowledge.

3. *Pitri yagna:* Contemplate the teachings of the forefathers, sages, saints and holy men and women as a reminder of the importance of preserving cultural heritage and values.

4. *Bhuta yagna:* Provide food for anyone in need, as an example of the spirit of sharing.

5. *Nara yagna:* Welcome and serve guests with respect and reverence (this is the core of the famed hospitality of Hindu households).

The Five Constant Duties

1. *Dharma (righteousness):* Live a virtuous life in accordance with the scriptures; be respectful of elders; perform the duties of everyday life for excellence rather than material reward.

2. *Tirthayatra (pilgrimage):* Visit temples, pilgrimage sites and holy people frequently, to provide freedom from routine life, enhance the mind and unify the family (all members should undertake pilgrimages).

3. *Utsava (holy days):* Join in festivals and holy days, both in the temple and at home. Observe fasts on holy days.

4. *Samskaras (sacraments):* Perform ceremonies as instructed in the scriptures to mark the passage through life.

5. *Sarva Brahma ("God is in all"):* Realize and live by the truth that God lives in the heart of all creatures.

• • • *HOW TO DOWSE* • • •

Dowsing is a method of searching for something hidden – whether household items, underground water, buried treasure or missing people. The skill of dowsing is said to be a sixth sense, which we all possess but seldom use. It can be fostered through practice with the use of rods or a pendulum. Here's how to start using rods:

1. Get a couple of coat hangers or some fencing wire and make two L-rods. They need not be elaborate – two simple L-shapes are all that is required, with the shorter arm of each one long enough to be held comfortably in the hand.

2. Loosely hold one rod in each hand, keeping both hands relaxed and shoulder-width apart. Your upper arms and forearms should form right angles with each other, your forearms and the rods parallel to the ground. This is the standard "search" position.

3. Decide on a simple target – anything at all for the time being. For example, the edge of a path or a particular stone or plant. Fix it in your mind's eye and channel your energy toward it.

4. Move around a little in the vicinity of your chosen target. When you reach the target, your rods ought to pick up on the energy you've been channelling toward it and change position. This often involves the rods swinging inward and crossing one another (although sometimes they swing outward). This movement is now your "found" signal. If, however, nothing happens, simply choose another target and try again.

5. Once you've established "found", start looking for things that you *really* want to find. Spend some time breathing deeply and visualizing your target before you begin. Be quietly confident that the rods will work – but also try not to set your expectations too high.

••• ❁ •••

• *THE FOUR KABBALISTIC WORLDS* •

Kabbalists believe the universe comprises four worlds or levels, which interpenetrate one another but get progressively further away from the divine. Referred to collectively as "Jacob's Ladder", in reference to Jacob's dream of a ladder ascending to heaven (Genesis 28: 11–19), the four worlds also relate to the stages of creation and to the Tree of Life (*see p113*). Below is an explanation of each world, including a summary of which *sephirot* on the Tree of Life they encompass:

1. **Atzilut (the world of emanation):** Symbolized by the element fire, this is the realm of pure spirit, of perfection, beyond time and space. It is the eternal, unchanging divine world at the top of the Tree of Life, encompassing the *sephirot* of both Kether and Chokmah.

2. Beriyah (the world of creation): Symbolized by the element water, this is the realm where form (matter) and force (energy) are brought into being. Male and female energies are polarized and start to bring order to chaos. This is the world of evolved souls, Messianic figures and creative possibilities. It is composed of the Binah *sephira* alone.

3. Yetzirah (the world of formation): Symbolized by the element air, this is the world of mental formulation, of psychic phenomena, and of angels and other intermediaries. We visit this realm in our sleep. It's where we find the heaven and hell of our own making. On the Tree of Life, it includes the *sephirot* of Chesed, Geburah, Tiphareth, Netzach, Hod and Yesod.

4. Assiah (the world of action): Symbolized by the element earth, this is the physical, material world in which we live. All sorts of things can be imagined and planned in the worlds above, but this is where they are brought into reality. It corresponds to the *sephira* Malchut on the Tree of Life.

••• ❁ •••

• • • CHILD'S POSE • • •

Balasana, or Child's Pose, is one if the most nurturing of all yoga *asanas*. Assuming the curled-up position acts as a subconscious reminder of the foetal position, creating feelings of extreme security and protection. It also encourages withdrawal of the senses (*pratyahara: see p32*).

Child's Pose is the perfect resting position between active phases in a yoga session (use it when you get tired) and is also a useful stress reliever in its own right. Practise it any time you feel stress or pressure building during your daily life: once you're in the position, imagine any tensions in your body flowing off your rounded back.

1. Kneel on the floor, with your buttocks on your heels. If this position is uncomfortable, place a cushion or folded blanket under your ankles, or between your feet and buttocks.

2. Roll your upper body forward, bringing your chest to your thighs and your forehead to the floor. Rest your head on a cushion or yoga block if it doesn't easily reach the floor. Enjoy the stretch in your hips, knees and ankles.

3. Relax your arms by your sides, palms up.

4. Stay in this position for between 30 seconds and a few minutes. Develop a deep awareness of your breathing by feeling the movement of your stomach against your thighs.

Caution: Pregnant women should avoid this pose.

• • • SOME TYPES OF GHOSTS • • •

Doppelgänger
Also known as a "fetch". A ghostly duplicate of a living person, it sometimes haunts its living counterpart. Seeing one brings bad luck.

Vardøger
In Norse mythology, a *vardøger* (meaning "forerunner") is a spirit double who moves before a living person, performing their actions in advance.

Gjenganger
In Scandinavian folklore, someone who has risen from their grave. Often violent or malicious in nature. Unlike most other ghosts, it's fully corporeal.

Poltergeist
A mischievous spirit that manifests itself by making noises and moving objects around. Not necessarily connected with a particular deceased person. It can work its mischief as an independent being, haunting a particular location.

Wraith
An apparition of a person, which may appear shortly before or after their death. Considered a bad omen. Typically depicted as a cloaked, faceless figure with a protruding hand, rather like the "Grim Reaper" in folklore.

• EIGHT ESSENTIAL ESSENTIAL OILS •

Aromatherapy oils can be used to treat a wide variety of everyday problems – via massage (*see p144*), baths or inhalations. Below are eight popular oils and the ailments that they most usefully address. All but two of them (lavender and tea tree) should always be diluted in a base oil, such as sweet almond oil, before use. Use eight drops of essential oil for every tablespoon (15ml) of base oil. Don't be tempted to use them undiluted – they are powerful and can cause negative side-effects.

Chamomile *(Roman or German):* For nervousness, depression, insomnia, teething in children, sunburn, rheumatism, eczema.

Geranium: For depression, insomnia, menopausal problems, chilblains.

Eucalyptus: For coughs, colds, cystitis, candida, sunburn.

Lavender: For burns and scalds, insomnia, depression and anxiety (can be used neat).

Lemon: For headaches, insect bites, veruccas, sluggish digestion.

Peppermint: For indigestion, headaches, migraine, fatigue, catarrh.

Rosemary*: For sprains, rheumatism, fatigue, headaches, coughs, colds.

Tea tree: For toothache, infections (ringworm, athlete's foot), acne (can be used neat).

*Caution: Anyone who suffers from epilepsy should avoid rosemary oil.

✛ ❈ ✛

• ECHIDNA'S MONSTROUS BROOD •

Described by the Greek poet Hesiod as a beautiful woman from the waist up but with the lower parts of a hideous serpent, Echidna was known as the "mother of monsters". Mating with Typhon, a hundred-headed giant created by the earth goddess Gaia to challenge Zeus, she gave birth to:

Cerberus, the fierce three-headed hound that guarded the Underworld (*see p37*)

The *Nemean Lion*, a fierce lion whose skin was impenetrable (*see p37*)

The *Chimera*, a fire-breathing lion-goat-serpent hybrid (*see p74*)

The *Lernean Hydra*, a multi-headed serpent-like swamp monster (*see p37*)

The *Sphinx*, a human-bull-lion-eagle hybrid, who preyed on the inhabitants of Thebes (*see p75*)

Orthrus, the giant Geryon's two-headed guard-dog (*see p37*)

••• ❀ •••

••• HINDU DENOMINATIONS AND THEIR ATTRIBUTES •••

Although the many denominations of Hinduism share fundamental beliefs and rituals, they all have slightly different emphases. Here are the three major traditions, and their associated deities and attributes:

TRADITION	PREDOMINANT DEITY	COLOUR	ASSOCIATED OFFERINGS	MAJOR SCRIPTURES	MANTRA
Shaivism	Shiva	Red	Roses, bilva leaves, *durva* (a grass)	*Vedas, Shaiva Agamas, Shaiva Puranas*	*Om Namah Shivaya*
Shaktism	Shakti (the goddess Devi, encompasses all the major Hindu goddesses)	Yellow (sometimes red)	Lotuses (to Lakshmi), yellow flowers (to Saraswati), red flowers (to Durga)	*Vedas, Shakta Agamas, Shakta Puranas*	*Om Hrim Chandi-kayai Namah*
Vaishnavism	Vishnu	White	White flowers, *tulsi* (holy basil) leaves	*Vedas, Vaishnava Agamas, Vaishnava Puranas, Ramayana, Mahabharata, Bhagavad Gita*	*Om Nara-yanaya*

. . . THE SIXTEEN REALMS . . .
OF BUDDHIST "HELL"

Buddhist cosmology encompasses a vast number of "worlds". The *Narakas* are the realms of suffering that equate to the Christian hell or, more accurately, to purgatory. If a person is born into one of these realms as a result of bad karma (*see p8*), this is not a permanent punishment – he or she may well be reborn into one of the higher worlds in the next life. Watched over by Yama, judge of the dead, the *Narakas* are not only physical places but also states of consciousness – and symbols of the suffering that can take place during life, as well as after death. There are various lists of *Narakas*, but this is one of the most common:

The Eight Cold Narakas

Arbuda (the Naraka of blisters): A dark, frozen plain surrounded by icy mountains, swept by blizzards. People live alone and naked, the extreme cold blistering their exposed bodies.

Nirarbuda (the Naraka of burnt blisters): Even colder than Arbuda. People's blisters burst open leaving bodies covered with frozen blood and pus.

Atata (the Naraka of shivering): People are so bitterly cold that they continually shiver, making an "at-at" sound (hence the name).

Hahava (the Naraka of lamentation): The extreme cold causes people to wail in pain, making the sound "haa-haa" (hence the name).

Huhuva (the Naraka of chattering teeth): With no respite from the cold, people shiver and their teeth are constantly chattering, making the sound "hu-hu" (hence the name).

Utpala (the "blue lotus'" Naraka): The intense cold makes people's skin turn blue like the colour of an utpala waterlily.

The Eight Hot Narakas

Sanjiva (the "reviving" Naraka): The ground is iron heated by a vast fire. People attack each other with iron claws. Yama's attendants attack with fiery weapons. Molten metal is dropped on people. Many are sliced into pieces.

Kalasutra (the "black thread" Naraka): As Sanjiva, but black lines are also drawn on the body, along which Yama's attendants cut with saws and axes.

Samghata (the "crushing" Naraka): Vast rocks come together, smashing people in between; when the rocks move apart, the bodies are revived, only to be crushed again.

Raurava (the "screaming" Naraka): People scream as they seek refuge (without success) from burning ground.

Maharaurava (the "great screaming" Naraka): As Raurava, but with greater suffering and more screaming.

Tapana (the "heating" Naraka): Yama's servants impale people on fiery spears until flames issue from their noses and mouths.

Cold (continued):
Padma (the "lotus" Naraka):
A blizzard rages, cracking open frozen skin and leaving bodies raw and bloody.

Mahapadma (the "great lotus" Naraka): People's whole bodies freeze and crack into pieces; their organs become exposed to the elements and crack. Extreme agony.

Hot (continued):
Pratapana (the "great heating" Naraka): People are impaled as in Tapana, but more bloodily still, as here Yama's servants use tridents to pierce their victims' bodies instead of spears.

Avici (the "uninterrupted" Naraka): People are continually roasted in an enormous fiery oven. Extreme agony.

••• ❈ •••

••• THE SEVEN CHARACTER ••• TYPES IN FOLKTALES

In the 1920s, the Russian scholar and literary critic **Vladimir Yakovlevich Propp** (1895–1970) analyzed a hundred Russian folktales, establishing that they all broadly contained a specific formulaic structure and that the characters within them could be grouped into just seven types. Although he published his findings in 1928 (in *Morphology of the Folktale*), it was only in the 1950s, when the book was translated, that scholars started applying Propp's analysis to folktales from other cultures, finding that the seven "types" he identified frequently held true. They can now be applied additionally to many modern stories and films:

1. The hero
The major character. Usually on a quest. Sometimes a victim or a seeker (after treasure or knowledge). Reacts to the donor [5]. Usually marries the prince or princess.

2. The helper
The character who helps the hero on his or her quest, providing practical support. Often has supernatural powers (example: a fairy godmother).

3. The dispatcher
The character who usually makes an initial misfortune or problem known, prompting the hero's journey.

4. The villain
The evil character who struggles against the hero, trying to prevent him or her from reaching the desired goal.

5. The donor
The character who gives the hero a special object (often a weapon or something with magical powers, or sometimes just good, old-fashioned advice).

6. The prince or princess, and his or her father
The character who presents the task to the hero, identifies the false hero and often marries the hero. Propp grouped these roles together as he felt that their function in any story was identical.

7. The false hero/ anti-hero/usurper
A character who tries to take credit for the hero's actions and/or tries to marry the prince/princess.